D1507680

Piedmont
College Library

Demorest, Ga.

86729

LC
1037.5
.E83

Essays on career
education and
English, K-12

370.11 Es7

Essays on Career Education
and English, K-12

NCTE Project on Career Education

Jan E. Kilby, Project Director
Charles Suhor, National Council of Teachers of English,
Administrative Director

Task Force on Career Education

Lori Clarke, University of Utah
Patricia Jo Clayton, Novelist, New Orleans, Louisiana
Marjorie N. Farmer, School District of Philadelphia
Edmund J. Farrell, University of Texas at Austin
Kris D. Gutierrez, University of Colorado
Marjorie M. Kaiser, University of Louisville
Glenn Leggett, President Emeritus, Grinnell College; Vice President, Deere
 and Company, Moline, Illinois, retired
Jesse Perry, San Diego City Schools
Donna Townsend, Texas Education Agency
Francis W. Weeks, University of Illinois at Urbana-Champaign

Essays on Career Education and English, K-12

Edited by

Marjorie M. Kaiser
University of Louisville

PB189   14

Project on Career Education
National Council of Teachers of English
1111 Kenyon Road, Urbana, Illinois 61801

Discrimination Prohibited. Title VI of the Civil Rights Act of 1964 states: "No person in the United States shall, on the ground of race, color, or national origin, be excluded from participation in, be denied the benefits of, or be subjected to discrimination under any program or activity receiving Federal financial assistance." Title IX of the Education Amendments of 1972, Public Law 92-318, states: "No person in the United States shall, on the basis of sex, be excluded from participation in, be denied the benefits of, or be subjected to discrimination under any education program or activity receiving Federal financial assistance." Therefore, career education projects supported under Sections 402 and 406 of the Education Amendments of 1974, like every program or activity receiving financial assistance from the U.S. Department of Health, Education, and Welfare, must be operated in compliance with these laws.

Consultant Readers: Carl McDaniels, Virginia Polytechnic Institute and State University; Seymour Yesner, Brookline, Massachusetts, School District

Book Design: Tom Kovacs, interior; V. Martin, cover.

NCTE Stock Number 15853

Published in 1980 and distributed exclusively by the National Council of Teachers of English, 1111 Kenyon Road, Urbana, Illinois 61801. Printed in the United States of America.

The material in this publication was prepared pursuant to a contract from the Office of Education, U.S. Department of Health, Education, and Welfare. However, points of view or opinions expressed do not necessarily represent policies or positions of the Office of Education.

Library of Congress Cataloging in Publication Data

Main entry under title:

Essays on career education and English, K–12.

    Includes bibliographies.
    1. Career education—United States—Addresses, essays, lectures. 2. English language—Study and teaching—United States—Addresses, essays, lectures. I. Kaiser, Marjorie, M., 1933–   II. National Council of Teachers of English. Project on Career Education.
LC1037.5.E83   370.11′3′0973   79-21408
ISBN 0-8141-1585-3

5/22/81 Buher + Tyler 6.50

Contents

Preface

This collection of essays, *Essays on Career Education and English, K-12*, is presented to the reader as being representative of the best, most positive expression by teachers at various levels on the subject of career education and the English language arts. Taken as a whole, the essays should acquaint preservice or beginning teachers with rationales and models for the integration of career education and language arts instruction in their curricula and classrooms. Experienced teachers will also welcome the drawing together of previously published articles and new essays, all focusing on the general topic of career education and English language arts.

The organization of the collection moves from the general to the specific. The essays in Part I address the issues of professional responsibilities; those in Part II offer justifications and recommendations for the integration of career education in the English language arts curriculum. Part III contains essays which present particular suggestions or teaching ideas for use in the classroom. Part IV consists of two articles which encourage us to think about the future. The reader in search of specific classroom strategies would do well not to ignore Parts I, II, and IV. Nearly every essay in the book contains teaching ideas. Further, while the emphasis in an individual essay may be on a particular grade level, English language arts teachers working at every level will find stimulating ideas and applications in every essay. For a wider selection of specific suggestions for classroom activities contributed by classroom teachers from all over the country, readers are urged to examine the companion to this volume, *Career Education and English, K-12: Ideas for Teaching.*

The editor takes this opportunity to express gratitude to all those who contributed to this volume by writing original essays, revising essays previously in print, or granting permission to reprint. For their leadership and sustained support, appreciation is due Jan Kilby, Project Director of the NCTE Project on Career

Education and English, and Charles Suhor, Administrative Director of the Project.

Marjorie M. Kaiser

Introduction

The term *career education* has been defined in various ways by leaders in the movement and by those in the academic disciplines since 1971. The official definition from the Office of Career Education and a clarification of some basic concepts related to it may aid the reader of this book.

Career education, as defined by the United States Office of Education, is "an effort aimed at refocusing American education and the actions of the broader community in ways that will help individuals acquire and utilize the knowledge, skills, and attitudes necessary for each to make work a meaningful, productive, and satisfying part of his or her way of living."[1] This definition should help make clear the distinction between career education and vocational education. Vocational education clearly refers to specific job preparation, whereas, as Kenneth Hoyt states, "career education is an attempt to impart to all students . . . those general employability skills that will allow students to change with change in the occupational society and to progress in that society."[2] These general employability skills include the following:

a. the basic academic skills of oral/written communication and mathematics;
b. good work habits;
c. personally meaningful work values;
d. understanding of and appreciation for the private enterprise system;
e. self-understanding and understanding of educational/occupational opportunities;
f. career decision-making skills;
g. job seeking/getting/holding skills;
h. skills in using unpaid work in productive use of leisure time; and
i. skills in overcoming bias and stereotyping as they impinge on full freedom of individual career choice.[3]

It should be obvious to teachers of the English language arts how most of these skills are intimately related to the standard goals and objectives of language arts instruction. There are two strategies which English language arts teachers can utilize in teaching their subject with a focus on career education.

Through the strategy of infusion, career education concepts are used as a means of motivating students to learn more of a subject itself. Through infusion we can aid our students in realizing the values of the skills and understandings we try to help them develop. Whether we are teaching composition skills, language study, or literary themes, a focus on the individual student's career development or on the meaning of work or on career development as a concept can add a new and purposeful dimension to the learning that occurs in our classrooms.

Through the strategy of collaboration, primarily with resources in the community, career education is used as a means to broaden students' knowledge of and insight into the world of work and to stimulate their learning through the provision of a wide variety of educational opportunities. By utilizing the community through field trips, interviews, and guest speakers, a language arts teacher can demonstrate how the study of the English language arts connects with the real-life practice of language skills and understandings.

Teaching the English language arts with a focus on career education *does not* imply that all objectives and classroom activities must be related to career education objectives. What it *does* imply is a forward-looking professional attitude on the part of the language arts teacher in striving to motivate all students to perform and understand to the best of their abilities this subject we call English language arts.

Background of This Publication

The 1978–1979 National Council of Teachers of English Project on Career Education and English, funded by the United States Office of Education, has inspired a renewed interest among NCTE members nationwide on this very important aspect of education in the seventies and eighties. Many individual members at all levels have long been concerned about the relationships between their efforts in the English language arts classroom and the world beyond that classroom. The Project has brought many of these individuals together—in person, working together as Task Force members and in convention sessions, and in various publications and communications.

But long before 1978, individuals and the leadership of NCTE evinced interest in career education and the teaching of the English language arts. As early as 1961, an NCTE Committee on Careers in English was established. This group, under the leadership of Elizabeth Berry, produced *The Careers of English Majors* in 1966. English and career education programs have been part of every national convention from 1971 through 1978.

In 1976, NCTE was invited to send representatives to a Mini-Conference on Career Education for Postsecondary and Association Representatives, sponsored by the United States Office of Education. An Ad Hoc Committee on Career Education was established to reexamine the interest in career education of English professionals and to attend the conference. During their meetings prior to the conference, members of the committee met to draw some conclusions about career education and to make some recommendations to the Council. The following is a list of their conclusions.

1. Career education in broad perspective is a proper concern for all English and language arts teachers.

2. Some of the things that go on in some English and language arts classes may be vocationally oriented—e.g., letter writing, learning to understand and fill out forms, and writing factual reports.

3. Much that goes on in English classes is career rather than vocation oriented: cognitive development, language acquisition and development, talking and listening, writing to communicate ideas or to clarify experience, strengthening reading skills, imagining oneself in alternate possible roles, and so forth. The outcomes of these activities will be valuable in a broad spectrum of occupations.

4. One of the most important contributions to career education through English is increasing confidence in the exercise of communication skills as a way of controlling and changing one's world.

5. The connection between some of the things that go on in English and language arts classes and career education may seem at times remote, tangential, or nonexistent. That, by itself, is no reason for discontinuing those activities (e.g., filmmaking by students who will probably never be employed as cinematographers, choral reading, writing limericks). There may be a connection, but we don't have to prove it to justify doing these things.

6. Although career education is a proper concern for English teachers, that matter has not received sufficient direct attention from NCTE.

7. Lack of attention leads to or stems from, or both, the lack of awareness or the reluctance to acknowledge, or both, on the part of English and language arts teachers, the responsibility they have toward the career education of their students.[4]

Most of these conclusions appear to remain points of agreement among the leaders and membership of the Council as they continue to examine their professional roles in the classroom and the community with special sensitivity to making English language arts instruction as meaningful as possible for all students. Teachers at all levels throughout the nation have produced a wealth of material illustrating a general professional concern for and a faith in the value of career education.

The establishment of the NCTE Project on Career Education and English has been effective in helping to focus the attention of the entire profession on this vital concern and to unify teachers of the English language arts on this important issue. As teachers have become more aware of the value of the philosophy and goals of career education and its natural connection to language arts instruction, they have become more and more comfortable with the concept. The authors of the essays in this collection consistently express *their* awareness of the great potential inherent in the integration of English and career education. Readers of the collection will surely share in their optimism about what this integration can do to revitalize language arts programs.

MK

Notes

1. Kenneth B. Hoyt, *A Primer for Career Education* (Washington, D.C.: Government Printing Office, 1977; Arlington, Va.: ERIC Document Reproduction Service, ED 145 252), p. 5.

2. Kenneth B. Hoyt, "The NCTE Career Education Project: Hopes and Aspirations," paper written for the National Council of Teachers of English, Urbana, Illinois, January 1979, p. 1.

3. Ibid., p. 2.

4. Minutes of the meeting of the Committee on Career Education of the National Council of Teachers of English, December 4-5, 1976.

I The Concerns
of English Professionals

Career Education: Implications for Teachers of English

Jan E. Kilby
NCTE Project on Career Education

This author asserts that English teachers can help students appreciate the value of English for *all* careers and can help them explore the many career opportunities in communications and media.

Someone once said that every new idea in education needs at least five years of clarification before it can be accepted.[1] It is now 1979, eight years since the concept of career education was formally introduced in 1971 by Sidney P. Marland, then commissioner of education at the United States Office of Education (USOE), and Kenneth B. Hoyt, then associate commissioner and now director of the Office of Career Education.[2]

After years of discussion, debate, and clarification of the concept of career education by school district personnel, staff members of the United States Office of Education and the Office of Career Education, state education department personnel, counselors, career development theorists, representatives of business, labor, and industry, and members of numerous professional associations for educators, career education has emerged, in fact, as a concept that is accepted as important by those concerned about education. The establishment of the Office of Career Education at USOE and the subsequent appropriations of funding through the Education Amendments of 1974 (PL 93-380) and the Career Education Incentive Act (PL 95-207) clearly confirm the commitment to career education by the public, members of congress, and the staff members of USOE.

As it is currently defined, career education is

an effort aimed at refocusing American education and the actions

This article was originally published in *English Education*, vol. 7 (Summer 1976), pp. 249-51. Copyright © 1976 by the National Council of Teachers of English. Reprinted by permission of the author and publisher.

of the broader community in ways that will help individuals acquire and utilize the knowledge, skills, and attitudes necessary for each to make work a meaningful, productive, and satisfying part of his or her way of living.[3]

Career education implies that all school personnel, in partnership with parents and members of community business, labor, and industry groups, share equal responsibility for facilitating the career development of all students, kindergarten through graduate or continuing education. The two primary strategies for integrating the career education concept into the school curriculum and program are infusion and collaboration. Through infusion, classroom teachers and other school personnel weave or "infuse" career education into the regular academic curriculum and school program. Through collaboration, educators, parents, and members of the community design learning materials and experiences to illustrate to students the close relationships between learning and career preparation.

All classroom teachers play an important part in career education. Their primary roles are helping students to see the value of the subject studied for their adult career and life roles and helping them to become acquainted with the specific career clusters and job opportunities related directly to the study of the subject.

For teachers of English on all levels, there are at least two major implications of career education. First, teachers of English can help students understand the value of effective communication skills for all the fifteen career clusters: agribusiness and natural resources; business and office; communications and media; consumer and homemaking education; construction; environment; fine arts and humanities; health, hospitality, and recreation; manufacturing; marine service; marketing and distribution; personal services; public service; and transportation. Students should see that reading, writing, speaking, and listening are part of every career. Second, teachers of English can expose students to the various occupations within the two career clusters directly related to the study of English: communications and media, and fine arts and humanities. A study of the many opportunities in journalism, technical writing, advertising, marketing, public relations, broadcasting, publishing, and printing can easily be incorporated into the English classroom.

If classroom teachers of English want to integrate career education into the curriculum with these two objectives in mind, the following guidelines are suggested.

1. Teachers can establish a departmental, schoolwide, or district-wide career education task force to share the responsibility for planning a comprehensive career education program. Such a group might perform the following tasks: develop level-specific objectives for career education; identify curriculum materials related to career development; establish contacts with professionals in the community who are engaged in communications-related careers in order to establish a speaker's bureau, a lay advisory council, or cooperative educational agreements for field experiences; and design in-service career education programs.

2. Teachers can acquaint themselves with the vast amount of career education materials for classroom use: films, posters, books, pamphlets, articles, journals, and government documents. To obtain such materials, teachers can contact their district supervisor of English language arts or specialist on career education, their state supervisor of language arts or their state career education coordinator, their school guidance specialists and librarians, personnel in their regional educational media/service center, and their professional associations.

3. Teachers can keep their knowledge of career development and career education current by attending inservice programs sponsored by their district or regional educational media/service center, by enrolling in graduate courses at colleges and universities, and by reading the research and literature on career development and career education.[4]

4. Teachers can acquaint themselves with the post-secondary educational opportunities in their communities, since students frequently seek information and guidance regarding their post-high school plans. Teachers can have on hand information related to vocational-technical institutes, community/junior colleges, four-year colleges and universities, apprenticeships, special programs of training offered by public and private organizations, and other forms of continuing education.

5. Teachers can provide opportunities to assist students in career awareness, career exploration, and career preparation as they study language, literature, composition, and film.[5]

6. Teachers should be continually aware of major political, social, and economic trends in society which have direct

implications for specific careers and should help students understand these implications.

7. Teachers can help students to understand that career development is a lifelong process involving many decisions and several major stages.

8. Teachers can help students to see careers realistically and to evaluate them in terms of working conditions, the nature of the work, salary, training and education required for entry and advancement, job security and outlook, value orientation, current and projected job hiring trends, and personality-related requirements.

All information provided to students should, of course, be accurate, up to date, and presented in a nonsexist manner. In fact, students should be encouraged to explore nontraditional careers.

Career education can be integrated easily into the English curriculum. Teachers can begin now to identify, collect, and develop methods, materials, and activities which will enhance the career development of the students in their English classes.

Notes

1. Dr. James W. Reynolds, Department of Curriculum and Instruction, University of Texas at Austin.

2. Sidney P. Marland, "Career Education," speech delivered at the National Association of Secondary School Principals' convention, Houston, Texas, January 23, 1971; "Marland on Career Education," *American Education* 7 (November 1971): 25-28. See also Kenneth B. Hoyt et al., *Career Education: What It Is and How to Do It* (Salt Lake City: Olympus, 1972, 1974); and Hoyt, *An Introduction to Career Education: A Policy Paper of the United States Office of Education* (Washington, D.C.: Government Printing Office, 1975; Arlington, Va.: ERIC Document Reproduction Service, ED 097 588).

3. Kenneth B. Hoyt, *A Primer for Career Education*, Monograph on Career Education (Washington, D.C.: Government Printing Office, 1977; Arlington, Va.: ERIC Document Reproduction Service, ED 145 252), p. 5.

4. Information is available from the ERIC Clearinghouse on Adult, Career, and Vocational Education, Ohio State University, 1960 Kenny Rd., Columbus, Ohio 43210. One may also write to the Office of Career Education, Room 3108, ROB #3, 7th and D. Sts. S.W., Washington, D.C. 20202.

5. Numerous articles, books, pamphlets, films, and government documents on the subject of English and career education are available. See Jan Kilby, *Career Education and English, K-12: Ideas for Teaching* (Urbana, Ill.: National Council of Teachers of English, 1980) for sample teaching ideas and a bibliography of curriculum resources.

Career Education
in the English Classroom

Dorothy Davidson, Texas Education Agency
Mildred Dougherty, Jefferson County, Kentucky, Public
   Schools
Marjorie Farmer, School District of Philadelphia
Jesse Perry, San Diego City Schools
Seymour Yesner, Brookline, Massachusetts, School District

This article explores in depth the relationships between career
education and the English language arts program. It addresses the
important question of balance between the humane and practical
uses of English. In addition to a thought-provoking discussion of
goals and issues, the authors offer sample exercises designed to
help achieve the specific goals they believe are legitimate for the
integration of career education and English.

We English teachers are constantly in the process of defining and
redefining the discipline that Americans call "English." During the
last decade, definitions have included (1) academic proficiencies—
language, literature, and composition; (2) fundamental skills—
listening, speaking, reading, and writing; and (3) basic communication competencies—literacy and verbal skills. By questioning its
own purposes, the English profession recognizes that work must
continually be reassessed, redirected, and reviewed as its living
context changes. And as the profession develops and employs this
capacity for self-assessment, with its implied dimension of freedom and courage to make changes as a result of new insights, the
process of definition becomes a significant element in any truly
comprehensive description of what "English" is.

But changes in definitions have not altered the profession's
core concerns. A primary concern is to give learners at the high

This article was originally published in *Career Education in the Academic
Classroom*, edited by James W. Becker and Garth L. Mangum, pp. 59-73.
Copyright © 1975 by Olympus Publishing Company. Revisions completed by
Marjorie Farmer and Mildred Dougherty. Reprinted by permission of the
authors and publisher.

school level an opportunity to achieve communication competencies that will equip them for the responsibilities of adulthood. A major responsibility of every adult is to do work that yields both personal fulfillment and service to the common good. Further, the English program seeks to prepare learners to participate creatively in the life of the world community. These are career purposes, and they are the purposes of the teaching of English.

As English teachers considering the career-oriented teaching of English, we have been trying to resolve for ourselves at least three major professional questions: (1) What is the relationship between the humane and the practical uses of English? (2) Where is the balance between our obligation to teach standard English and the importance of valuing linguistic differences? (3) What are the implications for the teaching of English of our students' varying career goals?

The task of reconciling the humane uses of English with its practical applications is basic in the profession. The humane uses are those experiences that help students define and enhance the self and achieve healthy interaction with others. These experiences are chiefly connected with literature and theater—the creative arts of language and communication. The practical uses are the means by which the self is presented and by which dynamic interaction with others is achieved. These are the specific skills needed for functional, practical literacy—the preparation of job applications and employment resumes and participation in interviews, public speaking, and other forms of informational and persuasive communication. An emphasis on career education in English can help clarify the interdependence of these humane and practical functions.

A related professional concern of English teachers is the maintenance of the necessary balance between the obligation to teach the conventions of standard, written, American English and the importance of valuing the varied linguistic styles of learners. English teachers increasingly are recognizing the interdependence of these two aspects of language. We understand that it is only on the underlying structure of each learner's unique "languaging" power, with its special style and content, that the learner can build a widening range of sophisticated linguistic strategies.

But the teaching decisions are not easy ones. If too much stress is placed on the practical aspects, the richness of various cultures and the interest of many persons in English studies may be lost. If too much stress is placed on the humanities, students may fail to learn skills that would enable them to communicate well with other people and that they may need in order to get certain types of work and to progress in their careers. Obviously, too, the profession must provide access to standard American English for learners from all language communities without denying the values and strengths of linguistic styles emerging from their own cultural heritages.

A third concern of the profession is to find ways to open career options to students in a manner that will prepare them equally well for higher education or for technical and other occupations. Past imbalances, arising from the emphasis on classroom work for the college-bound at the expense of that provided for the general student, were the result of the differential status historically assigned these groups in society and the fact that schools are run by people who themselves are products of higher education. But increasingly, financial rewards are being equalized among different types of employment, and greater regard is accorded the social contribution of each. Some of the factors that have helped bring about these changes are the numbers of middle class high school and college dropouts, welfare recipients' and prisoners' rights movements, fair employment practices, legislation establishing affirmative action requirements, efforts to provide compensatory education, more sophisticated labor-management negotiations, and the growing participation of people from all career groups in the processes of government.

As the English teaching profession addresses these questions, it does so in full awareness that high schools as they now exist often seem to fail in their services to the young. English, as a humane and liberating discipline, can make major contributions to the education profession by achieving a clearer sense of the equal dignity of all students and by helping young people find ways to achieve personal growth and motivation. Career education is an important medium for making these contributions.

What Is Career Education?

Career education concepts have contributed some new perspectives on the definition of a career. In the context of education, a "career" no longer refers only to a job that has a particular social stature, or one for which people have been specially trained, or one that is likely to be a person's livelihood for an entire lifetime. The word is not even limited to descriptions of work for which a person gets paid. Instead, the concept of "a career" now embodies—at least in the minds of career educators—far-reaching aspects of lifestyle, commitment, involvement, and self-fulfillment. While careers will still be regarded in the minds of some as being limited to that part of life connected solely with work, career educators see a career as being a continuing search for a satisfying and fulfilling life.

For the elementary and secondary school English teacher, these redefinitions in no way conflict with the intuitively perceived values underlying the work in English classes. In fact, if career education is the process by which individuals shape and control their destiny with some concurrent measures of personal satisfaction and social contribution, English should become a valuable resource to everyone because of the power it bestows on individuals to see into themselves and others and to manage their affairs competently and with affability. English also contributes in a more specific way to career education through its emphasis on communications skills. Most productive activities involve communication among human beings. Most instructions in paid employment must flow through spoken and written language. All human relations are communication. And all jobs that are not primarily manual are almost entirely based on communication—the transmission of ideas, orders, and messages.

To determine whether these career education needs of students are actually being met in the English classroom, one must appraise present teaching methods and content. Then the teacher can decide what should be continued, what should be altered, and what should be eliminated. Among the questions that should be raised in the course of this appraisal are the following:

1. Does instruction avoid an elitist bias: rather than favoring a small group of students, does it serve a broad student population well?

2. Does the teacher, by acknowledging and developing natural linguistic proclivities, help students develop their vocabularies, learn the subtleties of words, perceive relationships, stretch their minds, and engage in a variety of ways of thinking about their potential, their options, and the world in which they live?

3. Is the instruction so pertinent to experiences and events in everyday life that it is relevant to students' concerns and provides them with a way to interpret and express their own experiences?

4. Does the classroom develop skills that will enable students to argue ideas with themselves and with others in order to clarify their thinking and values and to resolve problems?

5. Are students achieving functional literacy—the ability to read and write according to their functional needs in school and in the world of work?

6. Is the English classroom helping students to know themselves and to know others, not just as fellow transients who pass this way but once, but as human beings with whom experiences and understanding are shared?

7. To cultivate such knowledge, is full use being made not only of literature but also of role playing, theater, and activities in such expressive areas as journalism, speech, debate, film, and dance?

8. Is English more than a simple tool for transmitting other subjects? Is it a base on which students can build realistic approximations of their social, vocational, and environmental roles, and will it help them make choices leading to satisfying and fulfilled lives?

When these questions can be answered in the affirmative, English becomes not a device for screening out students according to some prefabricated notion of winners and losers in collegiate or classical career terms, but a means for instructing all students in a purposeful, pleasurable classroom that uses the past and anticipates the future. We know that to say all this does not assure that English will be well taught or that methodology and content will always mesh in a manner that is perfectly and immediately clear to all students. But it is a probability, if not a certainty, that energizing students around their perceived interests and needs (even when these are self-centered or ultimately erroneous) will motivate them, help larger numbers of them find matters of consequence to themselves in the English classroom, and develop greater linguistic competence.

Career Education Goals

In incorporating career education in English studies, goals should be established that are aimed at helping students achieve economic independence, appreciate the dignity of work, learn about the satisfactions of work, and acquire the ability to make wise decisions about career options and choices. The following goals are for students who complete a high school English program. These students should obtain the following:

1. the communication understandings and skills necessary to become employable, to continue education throughout their lifetimes, and to pursue developing vocational and avocational career interests;

2. increased self-awareness and direction, expanded career awareness and aspirations, and appropriate attitudes about the personal and social significance of work and careers as a result of clarifying their values through literature and the other disciplines of English;

3. decision-making skills necessary for future long-range career planning, particularly in English-related careers and in other careers where linguistic ability is important.

The following sample objectives and learning activities may suggest to the English teacher how the content of the English program can facilitate the achievement of these goals.

Objectives for Goal One:
Developing Communication Skills Related to Careers

In the following exercises, students will (1) discover what it is like to work in various occupations related to English; (2) recognize that different kinds of written communication, ranging from simple messages to technical reports, are important components in various careers; (3) use language, spoken or written, in various ways, depending upon the purposes, situation, and audience; (4) experience vicariously a variety of roles through familiarity with literature that exemplifies different attitudes, values, and dilemmas of the human condition; and (5) make careful observations and interpretations of the content and language characteristics of various communications media, including films, radio, television, magazines, newsletters, newspapers, sales letters, posters and billboards, and public speeches.

Sample Exercises

Objective 1—Considering occupations related to English

a. Students will list the names of several characters in literature or persons in real life who have been successful in occupations related to English. By reading biographies, newspapers, or other research sources, students will obtain information that will enable them to describe at least some of the factors that led to the success of these persons.

b. Students will write research reports on occupations related to English, describing such matters as the range of opportunities in those fields, the number of persons now employed in these occupations, requisite skills and personal characteristics, educational and training requirements, pay, possibilities for promotion, advantages and disadvantages, work sites, degree of supervision and independence, and places in the community where such workers are employed.

c. Students will write essays illustrating the application of language study to careers of their choice. These essays should also include the reasons why they are interested in these careers, personal likes and dislikes that would affect their work in that career, their pertinent skills, and in-depth information on opportunities in the career field.

Objective 2—Recognizing many different kinds of written communication

a. Students will study specific occupations to determine the amount and the kind of reading and writing done; if possible, they should collect samples of writing by workers in these occupations.

b. Students will demonstrate an understanding of a variety of written communications in the world of work by producing an array of these communications and identifying where they are used and why they are needed.

c. Students will assemble and examine a variety of written communications from a single work site, such as a business office.

d. Students will evaluate the written communications of their peers as a means of strengthening their understanding of what they and their fellow students know and what must still be learned.

Objective 3—Using language, spoken and written, in different ways

a. Students will play roles and compare language in the following situations: class discussions, peer group discussions after school, student-adult discussions in a civic situation, and peer group interaction in a variety of social situations.

b. Students will produce samples of written language that are appropriate to different situations—from one class to another about a joint project, among peers about a social occasion, from adult to student to adult about a school issue.

c. Students will play roles in job interviews and in other career-oriented situations.

d. Students will discuss effective and ineffective uses of verbal and nonverbal communication.

e. Through interviews and other means, students will collect examples of the variety of interpersonal communication among workers in specific occupations.

f. Students will observe—by audiotape, film, or television, in offices or through simulations—various communication techniques used by adults in their work.

Objective 4—Experiencing a variety of roles through literature

a. Students will read fiction, essays, biographies, and autobiographies to determine how values and attitudes can shape decisions.

b. Students will analyze characters in their readings to discover the components of individual personality and the roles that these components play in human interaction.

Objective 5—Examining the uses of English in the communications media

a. Students will analyze uses of persuasive devices in the communications media.

b. Students will analyze political speeches that represent different viewpoints. They will report the facts presented, the weight given to various facts, and the interpretation of facts.

c. Students will participate in the filming or taping of a commercial or of a short narrative account of a football game, an accident, an environmental hazard, a school election campaign, or the like, and will adapt their presentations to subject content, media form, and audience.

Objectives for Goal Two:
Self-Understanding, Values, Definitions

In the five sample exercises below, students will (1) develop a systematic method to clarify their values; (2) demonstrate to what extent their values, abilities, interests, aptitudes, and attitudes are compatible with a variety of occupations and careers; (3) become aware of the personal significance that work and careers have for the individual; (4) learn ways that theater, film, radio, and other communications media offer a variety of experiences for personal growth, occupational satisfaction, and recreation; and (5) try to determine which values tend to be generative and to produce other values.

Sample Exercises

Objective 1—Developing a systematic method of clarifying values

a. Students will study a value hierarchy and illustrate it, using values discovered in a novel or short story. (Use the following format to show how values are built.)

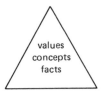

b. Students will apply a value hierarchy to situations set forth in the following: (1) a student-developed dialogue, (2) a filmed or taped commercial, (3) a magazine advertisement, (4) a television program, (5) a magazine article.

Objective 2—Considering values, abilities, interests, aptitudes, and attitudes in relation to occupations

a. Students will write essays illustrating the application of values, abilities, interests, aptitudes, and attitudes to specific career choices.

b. Each student will take an interest inventory, structure a profile, and analyze the profile for its accuracy in guiding him or her toward a career choice.

c. In a group effort, students will analyze the structure and content of an interest inventory.

Objective 3—Understanding the personal significance of work and careers

a. Students will analyze anecdotal accounts, such as newspaper interviews with interesting persons, to learn the personal significance of work and careers for various people.

    b. Through interviews, students will explore the differing values of individuals regarding their work; will invite guest speakers to the classroom; will view videotapes made at work sites.

    c. Students will write essays or participate in panel discussions on the role that a career plays in the development and nurturing of self-concepts.

Objective 4—Considering the relationships between nonprint media and personal growth, occupational satisfaction and recreation

    a. Students will role play, construct dialogues, and film and tape their dialogues, illustrating the value of nonprint media in personal growth and social diversion.

    b. Students will explore facilities in the community, including an educational television studio, different kinds of movie houses and radio stations, and community theater groups.

Objective 5—Examining values that produce other values. Students will assess statements like the following in terms of how they can generate additional values.

    a. Seeking goals and answers to problems is a person's destiny and should be construed as valuable and pleasurable in itself.

    b. Knowing about the world as realistically as possible is good.

    c. Having the power to express oneself according to one's urges and needs is self-enhancing.

    d. The ability to project one's understanding into the lives of others is powerfully liberating and self-sustaining.

    e. Being able to identify imaginatively and sympathetically with others and with their problems is revitalizing.

    f. The ability to communicate with others sustains one's own sense of worth and assures one's place in a community.

    g. Having a sense of security as a result of work, social place, and communication with other people reduces social apprehension and alienation.

Objectives for Goal Three:
Developing Decision-Making Skills

The objectives for this goal are threefold: (1) to make and analyze career decisions on the basis of a decision-making model that includes consideration of rewards, costs, alternatives, and personal values; (2) to be able to gather information regarding a career choice through reading, interviewing, observing, and other communicative means; and (3) to be able to use one's knowledge of oneself and of various careers to make tentative career choices.

Sample Exercises

Objective 1—Making and analyzing career decisions

a. Students will choose occupations in which there are generalists and specialists, interview these workers in terms of job satisfactions and dissatisfactions, and write an analysis of their findings.

b. Students will search for answers to such questions as: (1) What do newspaper reporters and printers do? (2) How do they write, edit, and print the news? (3) What do other staff members do?

c. Students will visit a local newspaper establishment to talk to workers, examine the newspaper, and produce a class report on careers in journalism.

Objective 2—Gathering information on career choices

a. Students will interview adult workers and describe how life experiences have affected their career development.

b. Students will locate sources of information on selected careers, including the school library and school counseling office and sources in the community—private and public employment agencies, computerized information services, vocational education centers, and community colleges.

Objective 3—Using knowledge of oneself and of careers to make tentative career choices

a. Each student will prepare a personal resume and/or a portfolio that includes creative or informative writing and other types of communications (photo essays, cartoons, graphics) that may be useful in helping parents, counselors, vocational educators, prospective employers, or college entrance interviewers aid in the determination of appropriate career channels and choices.

b. Students will be encouraged to use language in appropriate classroom situations so as to gain experience in speaking effectively about their career interests and their personal strengths.

Implementation Strategies

How should the English teacher go about developing a career-oriented curriculum of this kind? Of course, the individual teacher may work apart from colleagues, incorporating into course plans ideas gained from this essay and from other sources. But the going may be easier if the teacher works with colleagues within the English department and across departmental lines, particularly if the school has outside consultation services, a library of resource materials, and other supports for a curriculum development program. But whether the teacher works alone or with others, the following steps are appropriate in implementing career education goals in the English classroom.

First, formulate goals, objectives, expected outcomes, and evaluation plans. A number of resources may be drawn upon—guides from other schools, bulletins developed in state departments of education and career education projects, articles in the *English Journal* and other professional magazines, and the like.

Second, identify instructional resources. The English teacher may know the community served by the school and may be able to identify individuals, groups, businesses, industries, professional and service organizations, and institutions that can provide information useful to students. There may be available a master list of community resources from which to draw much of this information. Students themselves are an important resource, and their involvement in planning, sharing, and developing ideas on career education in the English classroom should be used creatively.

Teachers from vocational education, social studies, fine arts, foreign languages, and other disciplines should be added to the resource pool. Parents and other family members are also sources of information on a wide variety of occupations and on career values, aspirations, and decision-making processes. These efforts may result not only in a good career education program but also in profitable lines of communication between the English classroom and other departments in the school and between the school and the community.

Third, make decisions on program elements. Having established goals, objectives, expected outcomes, and evaluation plans for a career-oriented program, the English teacher is ready to decide on the changes needed in the organization and content of existing courses. New courses may also be needed, although the infusion of career education concepts in all courses, new or old, is more readily defensible than adding a new course to the school curriculum—and it will probably accomplish more.

If the implementation effort includes the entire school, English teachers should participate in making decisions about staffing. Alternative staffing patterns may build upon the strengths and competencies of individual teachers. Team teaching and cooperative arrangements crossing departmental lines for both planning and teaching may make the best use of competencies. Resource persons from the community may further enrich the instructional plans. The objective should be to seek out and find ways to use the best possible persons, supplementing the competencies of each English teacher and broadening the perspectives of students through real-life experiences relating to careers, work-oriented values, and career decision making.

The English teacher engaged in the process of developing a career-oriented program should also explore how a single broadening of perspective can help bring about a good career education focus. For example, in connection with the various strategies that the teacher already uses to explore a student's interests, background of experience, values, attitudes, and competence in the language arts, the teacher might also begin to gather information, observations, and impressions that are important to career development. What work experiences have individual students had? What are their views of work? What are their career aspirations at the moment? Answers to these and other questions begin to round out the English teacher's view of each student, and this can serve as a basis for individualizing plans for a career-oriented program.

Summary

While the teaching of English undergoes continual redefinition, its inherent purpose is steadfast: to give students the opportunity to achieve communication competencies that will serve them as adults in seeking personal fulfillment, in giving service to the common good, and in participating creatively and effectively in the life of the community. Career education, broadly defined, can help us revitalize the content and the methodology of the school English program at a time when students are seeking clarification of their personal values and are facing the need to make career decisions. The English classroom can become a laboratory in which learners explore communication in its many forms and prepare for a lifetime of effective and satisfying communication with other people. These are vital skills, for they are used in work, in leisure, and throughout the whole of life in the human community.

Selected References

Barnes, S. J. *Creative Behavior Guidebook.* New York: Scribner's, 1967.

Gordon, W. J. J. *The Metaphorical Way of Learning and Knowing.* Cambridge, Mass.: Porpoise Books, 1971.

Hawley, Robert C., et al. *Composition for Personal Growth: Values Clarification through Writing.* New York: Hart, 1973.

Judging from Language. 16mm, 20 minutes. Washington, D.C.: Bono Film Services. The film raises questions about the effects of a nonprestige dialect in a job interview, but it offers no answers.

Prince, G. M. *The Practice of Creativity: A Manual for Dyanmic Group Problem Solving.* Evanston, Ill.: Harper & Row, 1970.

Raths, L., et al. *Values and Teaching: Working with Values in the Classroom.* Columbus, Ohio: Charles E. Merrill, 1966.

Shaftel, Fannie. *Role-Playing for Social Values.* Englewood Cliffs, N.J.: Prentice-Hall, 1972.

Washington State Coordination Council for Occupational Education. *Who Am I? Where Am I Going? How Do I Get There? A Guide for Career Awareness.* Seattle: Washington State Coordination Council for Occupational Education.

II Career Education and the English Curriculum

Goals of Career Education and Goals of English Language Arts Instruction: A Model

Charles Suhor
National Council of Teachers of English

The author focuses on the concepts of congruent, overlapping, and distinctive goals for English language arts and career education. He believes that many of the cognitive and affective goals of language arts instruction are congruent with career education goals and that teachers and curriculum developers need to plan carefully to utilize these areas of overlap.

Advocates of career education have long held that they are not championing a new discipline or distinct area of specialization. Career education is not seen as a new area added on to present school programs but as a concept to be infused in existing curricula. Still, many English language arts teachers tend to see career education as an invasion of their subject matter area. We need to clarify the relationships between the goals of career education and the goals of language arts instruction so that teachers and curriculum developers can work with a conscious knowledge of what does and does not have career relevance.

There are two unproductive ways of looking at career education and English. One is to state that *all* education is relevant to careers. Such a claim invites no changes in instruction at all, since it implies—incorrectly, I believe—that everything we do in language arts instruction is, in fact, rich in career implications. The other unproductive approach is to generate a limited repertoire of career-oriented units for use in English classes in order to "cover" career concerns. This strategy supports the idea that career education is, after all, a series of artifices grafted onto "real" subject-area content.

This article is adapted from "Goals of Career Education and Goals of Subject-Area Instruction: A Model," *Journal of Career Education*, vol. 5 (March 1979), pp. 215-19. Copyright the Curators of the University of Missouri, 1979. Reprinted by permission of the author and publisher.

23

If language arts teachers at all levels are to give a genuine career focus to their programs, we must develop a clear concept of the relationships among career education goals and those of language arts instruction. The models presented below explore these relationships in graphic form, representing English language arts goals as a dotted square and career education goals as a square composed of diagonal lines (Figure 1).

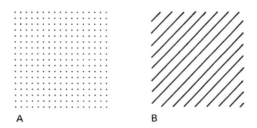

A　　　　　　　　　　B

Figure 1.　Subject-Area Goals (A) and Career Education Goals (B)

Certain goals of career education and subject-area instruction will be viewed as *congruent;* others as *overlapping;* still others as essentially *distinctive.*

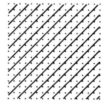

Figure 2.　Congruent Goals

In Figure 2, career education goals and English language arts goals are *congruent*—that is, the subject-area goals and the career goals match exactly. Such goals are generally closely related to fundamental skills in thinking, listening, speaking, and writing. For example, critical thinking skills taught in English classes will have direct application in a wide variety of careers that require the critical analysis of ideas. Skill in large and small-group discussion is another language arts goal that is valuable in most careers. Skill in writing is also important to advancement in many career areas.

Students trained in these process-oriented skills become, *ipso facto*, trainable—and the trainable employee is well suited for life in a society of rapidly changing occupations.

College teachers of methods courses can use the concept of congruent goals to refocus attention on the intellectual processes underlying a discipline. Too often, the main goal of subject-centered instruction is the mere imparting of information. The congruent goals model, in addition to suggesting the intimate connection between career education and major language arts goals, underlines the importance of a process approach to language arts instruction. Of course, I've listed here only a few examples of congruent goals. A large list of such goals and related activities might be created for language arts instruction. Curriculum developers recognize that an increased stock of congruent goals would greatly enrich both career education and the overall design into which career concepts are infused.

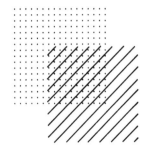

Figure 3.   Overlapping Goals (Subject-Based)

Figure 3 represents an *overlapping* of language arts goals and career education goals in an instructional unit that is fundamentally *subject-based*. While the dominant focus of the unit is on skills, themes, topics, and so forth, in language arts, the points of overlap are seen as natural extensions of the unit and not contrivances. For example, a study of the techniques of persuasion or propaganda in English might be enriched by visits to a television newsroom and an advertising agency, with an examination of the various work roles involved. Study of literary works, from *The Canterbury Tales* to *Death of a Salesman*, might include discussion of the authors' views of the world of work. Free writing might include students' reactions to topics like, "If I were a . . . [student's choice of a job] " or, "Three jobs I would [like/not like] to have."

Teachers with extensive graduate level training in their subject areas are sometimes suspicious of a career education emphasis, seeing it as intrusive, if not downright anti-academic. But when career activities are planned as a natural outgrowth of the ongoing instructional program, fears about poaching and trivialization disappear. Few people are so narrow as to totally deny the educational and motivational value of real-world applications of the study of their discipline.

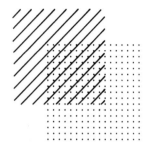

Figure 4.   Overlapping Goals (Career-Based)

In Figure 4, a *career-based overlap* exists. Here a career unit is devised, but it inherently involves a mastery of certain language arts skills. For example, English students might answer classified ads, thereby exercising composition skills and demonstrating letter-writing form. In role-playing job interviews, students imaginatively project themselves into new situations, thus supporting the broader goals of language and literature programs. An annual Career Day program might be used as a research project in which students select a career area, write a job description, and comment on their feelings about such work.

Instructional units that have overlapping goals—whether these are subject-based or career-based—can be created by thoughtful classroom teachers. The development of such units is not a matter of training one's ingenuity but of finding logical ways to extend subject-matter concerns on the one hand, and to make use of the discipline-related aspects of career activities on the other. A strained, overingenious linking of career and language arts concepts would result not in infusion, but confusion.

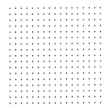

Figure 5. Distinctive Goals

Figure 5 constitutes a frank admission that some language arts goals are their own excuse for being—that is, they are *distinctive*, having no apparent career relevance except for the student who might later become a language arts specialist—an English teacher, editor, lexicographer, or poet, for example. Scanning the meter of a Petrarchan sonnet is of little use to anyone except the potential English scholar. Knowing the definition of a diphthong, participial phrase, or oxymoron is not relevant to most careers, nor is the ability to diagram a sentence or discover recurring images in a poem. Moreover, the learning of these skills is not normally within the basic process orientation described in the congruent goals model.

No doubt many distinctive goals are an important part of the liberal education of students in our society. Not every goal need be career-related, or utilitarian in other ways, for that matter. But distinctive goals in language arts instruction should be carefully examined by teachers, curriculum developers, and administrators. There is a genuine question as to whether *all* students should be given intensive study in the esoterica of our discipline. For example, many English specialists are increasingly concerned that students who might otherwise enjoy poetry are put off by academic exercises in scansion or by tortured analyses of imagery.

One productive outcome of using the models above might be the discovery of the distribution of *kinds* of goals in a given lesson plan, course of study, or curriculum. The presence of a large number of distinctive goals might suggest that educational priorities are misplaced, focusing excessively on the subject rather than on the student. A well-balanced program in the English language arts would probably be strong on congruent goals, reflecting a double orientation towards both the cognitive and career development of the student; rich in overlapping goals, reflecting a sense of connectedness between language arts instruction and the world of work; and highly selective in distinctive goals, reflecting a thoughtful approach to the student's liberal education rather than indiscriminate dumping of specialized concepts into the curriculum.

Whether or not the present career education movement persists as a national effort, the individual teacher will continue to face the problem of bringing subject matter instruction into a proper relationship with students' career needs and goals. The models above are an attempt to provide a framework for analyzing that problem in a coherent way. The analysis aims at sorting out language arts and career education goals, establishing relationships between them, and implicitly reassessing goals in the process.

Reading Requirements
for Satisfactory Careers

Beatrice J. Levin
School District of Philadelphia

Focusing on the relevance of reading and general literacy to work
of all kinds, this author outlines the specific reading and study
skills essential to performance in our career-oriented society. In
addition, the author suggests steps for relating the reading content of a particular discipline to career education.

Career education has been described as a concept whose time has
come. However, many of its components have long been parts of
educational programs. The idea of career education is new only in
the way these elements have been reorganized, restructured, and
applied to permeate the entire educational system. Career education is a holistic concept which includes both job satisfaction and
the imaginative use of leisure; it involves all members of the
school family—superintendent, principal, teacher, counselor—as
well as the community at large. It facilitates education of all students so that they may appropriately choose and prepare for their
life's work as well as all aspects of living. Broader than the concept
of vocational education, it subsumes all career possibilities for
students, from occupational job entry at high school graduation to
more technical or professional careers requiring additional schooling. Career education's underlying appeal lies in its acceptance of
all genuinely productive human endeavor as worthy and creditable
and its realistic development of this attitude through the educative
process. Since it has met with such immediate nationwide enthusiasm, it appears urgent that some of our educational priorities be
reordered and the curricula dissected to determine career education's relevance to the needs of today's students. In order to

This article was originally published in *Reading and Career Education,*
edited by Duane M. Nielsen and Howard F. Hjelm, pp. 77-81. Copyright
© 1975 by the International Reading Association. Reprinted by permission
of the author and publisher.

prevent career education from becoming just another passing educational fad, its philosophy must be thoroughly understood and integrated in the total instructional program so that education will be revitalized and more responsive to the demands of this rapidly changing world.

It is a dereliction of duty on the part of educators to fail to introduce students to and prepare them for the wide variety of career options open to them. Through career education and training, students can achieve economic independence and personal and social satisfaction.

Importance of Reading

Career education subsumes the attainment of personal gratification not only through a sense of achievement at dignified work, but through development of a broader humanistic involvement in community affairs and the creative use of leisure time. Since the development of vocational and intellectual skills pervades all subject areas, the need for good reading skills is axiomatic. There are no areas in either the academic world or the world of work in which reading does not play a crucial role. Even at the lowest job entry level, people have to be able to read and follow directions in order to complete simple tasks correctly, read and fill out applications and other forms intelligently, and read newspapers and periodicals with adequate understanding to make intelligent, independent judgments on political and social issues. Whether they are following the sequence of steps in a job sheet or studying a text on constitutional law, they must be able to understand and correctly interpret the printed word at whatever level of abstraction it is written.

The ultimate aim of education is to produce in learners independence with which to (1) earn a living according to their interests and abilities, (2) think and act creatively as citizens of the world community, (3) pursue avocational and recreational activities, and (4) continue lifetime learning. Capabilities for continuous learning are particularly important in a changing world requiring adaptation to a variety of altered conditions. Undoubtedly, people now entering the job market will have to make numerous adaptive occupational changes and personal adjustments during their lives; this spiral of change in social and economic structures places an even greater emphasis on the need for effective reading-thinking skills. Because knowledge and the written records thereof are increasing at breakneck speed, students cannot learn all there is to know in the course of their school years in elementary, secondary, college, and graduate school. The process skills of reading— knowing how and where to find needed information; how to read it evaluatively in terms of its pertinence to a particular need; how to organize this information so that it is manageable, logical, and easily retrievable; and how to retain those elements that are most essential—assume greater importance than the content of any one subject. Reading educators must teach students to skim when looking for a particular fact or piece of information, to read rapidly when only a general idea of the material is needed, and to lessen the reading pace when the material is loaded with information or technical language that requires more intensive reading. Mere exposure to printed facts without teacher direction for relating and organizing contributes little to the development of the essential thinking-reasoning process. To develop these cognitive processes, teachers must help students (1) determine main ideas in printed materials and verify that these ideas are extracted from and supported by the stated facts, (2) make logical inferences by reading between the lines where there is factual evidence to give it credence, (3) perceive the difference between fact and opinion, and (4) become familiar with propaganda devices and discriminate between connotative and denotative language. All of these skills are essential in a career-oriented society.

Reading skills needed at the lower levels of job entry involve the literal interpretation of texts. In the vocational-occupational area, for example, essential skills are understanding printed directions, following the steps in a sequence, learning a basic sight vocabulary of the technical terms in a given vocation, finding the main idea, noting specific details, and using the dictionary and other resource materials. Recently, a group of vocational-occupational teachers in a comprehensive high school exhibited an interest in learning how to help their students read the technical materials in their areas, admitting that most books and job sheets are overloaded with difficult technical terms. An analysis was made of some of the materials, listing specific skills needed to read them comprehensively. Following an examination of the vocabularies, suggestions were made for reinforcing new and difficult terms via graphic illustrations, filmstrips, class-made flip cards, labeling, display and bulletin boards, and word of the day. Most of the required skills revolve around following directions in a sequence of steps where comprehension is immediately tested in the product or outcome.

An electronics teacher wanted to teach his students to do critical reading, make intelligent inferences, and draw reasonable conclusions from facts stated in electronics materials. Thus, even at the lower job entry levels, good critical reading-reasoning skills are desirable for both adequate job performance and personal development.

Students must be made aware that reading plays a vital role in enhancing or impeding their plans for immediate or ultimate job entry; they must know that reading is not an abstract intellectual option but is as necessary a tool for the auto mechanic as for the engineer, historian, or lawyer. In addition, teachers and administrators have an important role in preparing students to function at the highest reading level of which they are capable.

Students need the whole range of literacy skills in order to make career and vocational choices freely. Basic reading and study skills which all students should acquire during their years of schooling are:

1. *Word-attack skills*

   Extensive sight vocabulary
   Phonic analysis
   Using context clues
   Syllabication
   Knowledge of compound words
   Recognizing roots, prefixes, suffixes, and inflectional endings

2. *Word-meaning skills*

   Understanding technical terms
   Using the glossary
   Using the dictionary
   Using new terms in speaking and writing
   Understanding figurative language
   Understanding denotations and connotations of words

3. *Comprehension skills*

   Determining main ideas, whether explicit or implicit
   Selecting relevant details
   Recognizing relationships among main ideas
   Organizing ideas in sequence
   Understanding time and distance concepts
   Following directions
   Reading maps, tables, and other graphic material
   Distinguishing between facts and opinions

Making judgments
Drawing inferences and giving supporting evidence

4. *Study skills*

Outlining
Taking notes
Scheduling time efficiently
Preparing for examinations
Preparing for discussions and reports
Using reference materials
Adjusting rate of reading to suit purpose and content

Staff development in career education must consider the dual purpose of reading—for information and recreation. Students who are having difficulty with reading tend to be motivated by reading material related to a job-oriented task. The following steps are advocated for relating the reading content of a particular discipline to career education.

1. Determine the general skills needed for students to master the subject content.

2. List specific reading skills needed to comprehend the subject area materials.

3. Set up a sequence of educational objectives based on steps 1 and 2.

4. Evaluate students' reading levels and needs (via informal inventories, past records, word-attack surveys, vocabulary checks, anecdoted records, standardized tests).

5. Match the materials to the instructional levels of the students; group the class flexibly to provide for individual reading needs and strengths.

6. Plan instructional strategies to eradicate students' deficits and provide for increased development and refinement of skills.

7. Include listening, speaking, and writing activities because of their interdependence with reading.

8. Encourage free reading at specified intervals by providing saturation with other related reading materials (e.g., a classroom paperback library).

9. Provide appropriate evaluation as an ongoing, integral part of the instructional program.

10. Include good questioning techniques which stimulate stu-

dents to think creatively and critically, to evaluate what they read, to organize facts into a meaningful whole, and to make intelligent judgments based on sound evidence. Undoubtedly, the kinds of questions posed by the teacher influence the kinds of thinking students do.

11. Provide precise and extensive vocabulary development activities.

Conclusion

It has been estimated that one-third of our nation's youths leave school without obtaining sufficient reading skills to meet the demands of employment. These young people emerge into the adult world with little sense of personal worth, with social and vocational inadequacies, and with overriding feelings of hopelessness and futility. Many junior and senior high school students fall into this category; their deficits in reading and general literacy depress their accomplishments in both academic and vocational-occupational areas. As a student advances through the grades, it is progressively more difficult to fail in reading and yet succeed in other educational endeavors. With the sophisticated demands of a technological society, there is no place for the inadequate reader—the technician who cannot translate technical material into comprehensible action, the secretary whose language skills are inadequate for appropriate communication, or the economist who cannot properly interpret present trends in the light of the historical past.

To prepare students for a future likely to contain lightning and unchartered change, survival may depend on such skills as the ability to communicate at all levels, competency in solving problems through creative and divergent thinking, and management of a vast conglomerate of steadily burgeoning knowledge. Indispensable to the acquisition of those skills is the exceedingly complex, interwoven set of skills and processes known as reading.

In Addition to Skills, What?

Alan Lemke
University of Nebraska at Lincoln

This author urges English teachers to look more closely at their programs to determine the "effectiveness and smoothness" with which the teaching of career education and the study of English can occur. The author stresses the utilitarian uses of English and the importance of making meaningful contacts with the community, but he also proposes ways that instruction in skills can be extended to deal with the larger issues of the English curriculum.

A few years ago in St. Louis, William Walker, who was at that time the director of the Atlanta, Georgia, Office of Economic Opportunity, spoke about the integration of career education and the teaching of language arts, especially those facets of language arts lying beyond basic skills. Once the business letters have been written, job application forms filled out, the newspaper diction mastered, and the stage fright controlled, what does English have to offer young people and a nation losing faith in liberal education as prerequisite experience to intelligent and comfortable living?

William Walker's question captures the attention of English teachers interested in or fearful of integrating the teaching of English and career education. In addition to the skills, what? This essay provides two answers. First, in addition to and while teaching language arts skills through the use of community resources, teachers of English should lead students in the *study* of language, literature, and composition. Second, the teaching of language arts skills and the study of language, literature, and composition should occur simultaneously. Both the question, "In addition to the skills, what?" and the answers are neither new nor shocking. Professional literature on the integration of English and

This article was originally published in *The Leaflet*, vol. 74 (Fall 1975), pp. 20-27. Copyright © 1975 by the New England Association of Teachers of English. Reprinted by permission of the author and publisher.

career education has not yet recognized the effectiveness and smoothness with which the teaching of skills and the study of English can occur.

Before it addresses the integration of career education, the teaching of language arts skills, and the study of language, literature, and composition, an English program must meet three prerequisite conditions. (1) Teachers of English, career education specialists, vocational education teachers, guidance counselors, and students must realize that "career English" is not a synonym for vocational English, dummy English, or relevant English. Career English is English for all students. (2) The English curriculum must be at least crudely progressive, such that students recognize differences in academic depth in English class, year after year. Students of English in high school must not experience each English class as one more opportunity to learn the use of the comma, the use of models of deductive and inductive paragraphs, and the use of the moralist's or the formalist's approach to literature. (3) English teachers must be willing to take seriously the problems of the poorly educated, especially those looking toward years of unrewarding work and unemployment in a repressive society. An English curriculum in which these conditions are no more than wishful thinking is not yet ready either to address itself to career education or to complain about having to make English relevant to the world of work. (Although these three conditions are significant and crucial, their mention here is not meant to overlook the enthusiasm and ability of English teachers, the enthusiasm of students, and the support of the general public.) Like the teaching of English, career education will flourish in the best climates, grow briefly but never bear fruit in better climates, and wilt in poor climates.

In relation to language arts and to career education, the question, "In addition to the skills, what?" covers more than can be addressed comprehensively in a single essay. Readers are encouraged to consider all the activities described in the rest of this essay and in other essays as examples of ways to integrate the study of language with both the least and the most exciting aspects of career education and English. It follows that this essay ought to focus on something as routine as the teaching of the business letter and, on the other hand, on the teaching of literature. English teachers who understand and improve on the examples in this essay will comfortably integrate career education and English in other areas of the English curriculum. I have deliberately chosen simple examples and have stayed with them long enough to show a number of variations.

Career education manifests a concern for the utilitarian uses of language; and once during school years, students of language and composition spend time wisely if they study the uses, format, and exemplary contents of business letters. Once is enough if the job is done well. Letters of inquiry concerning possible employment, letters written in response to the reception of damaged or defective merchandise, letters requesting travel information—all these should be examined and written during the junior high years. Together, teachers and students can think of many kinds of business letters to write and study.

What does it mean to *study* business letters and at the same time study language? In addition to learning the skills, what? While students learn and practice dozens of letter writing skills, teachers who are worth their salt and wish to integrate the teaching of language arts and career education can do a little extra because they are more interested in what students think than in what students can do. In schools, performance is important, but not nearly as important as understanding *what* one does and *why* he or she does it. Only then can a far more important question be asked: "Do I want to do it?" Suppose junior high students, who had just learned the rigors of doing everything just right in business letters, were asked to write the following: (1) the first paragraph of a business letter to a Datsun regional service manager, whose name they have; (2) the first paragraph of a business letter to a local Datsun service manager who has visited the class or who has been described carefully by the teacher; and (3) the first paragraph of a business letter to the local Datsun service manager, each student assuming that his or her favorite uncle is the service manager. By agreement, the content of all the letters would be about the same problem. The first letter would be written without students' knowing that the others are to be written, and perhaps not all students would write all three letters. Students would be carefully instructed to explain the situation in a way that the receiver of the letter would like. Letters would be shared once they were all written. Once editing problems were taken care of so that all good letter writing skills had been practiced and learned at a high level of excellence, the question of a writer's audience could be raised. What effect does a writer's audience have upon writing style? Do the three letters reveal identical, similar, or quite different styles? If students need help noticing differences, teachers can state their impressions of differences in syntax, diction, tone, sentence length, and so on among the three letters. For example, if the letters are to be ones of either mild or vicious complaint, students can compare the uses of words whose emphases are carried in their denotative meanings with uses of words whose emphases are carried in their connotative meanings. Teachers might find that emotive language is used or not used depending upon the audience for the letters. These elementary but crucial issues in rhetoric and semantics need not take second place to the practice of language skills in business letters if teachers will ask, "In addition to skills, what?" Neither do these principles of rhetoric and semantics have to be taught in a vacuum without reference to the world outside the school or without reference to a student's own use of language.

Studying and understanding business letters includes thought about such student questions as, "Why can't I have the kind of margins I like?" or "Why is my letter so boring?" Suppose two or three students were to call a local banker, a service manager for Sears, a state English consultant, or a busy insurance office receptionist and ask questions about how many letters are read each day, how those letters are answered, and what it feels like to be a letter answerer. Suppose two or three students were assigned the task of answering all the letters to the regional Datsun service manager. These and similar activities would illustrate the role that similarity, pattern, and strict adherence to format play in the toleration and efficient answering of letters from complaining customers. Until students understand the reasons for the rigors of the business letter format, they will not know the differences between training and education, policing and teaching, and not liking and liking learning.

Educated and experienced teachers of English can extend the letter writing exercise still further into the study of rhetoric, semantics, composition, or dialectology. The writing of business letters should be done in such a way that students not only learn language skills and business letter format, but simultaneously learn the principles of semantics, rhetoric, and dialectology. The enthusiastic integration of career education and English facilitates such learning and teaching without striking fear in the hearts of English teachers who wish to maintain high academic standards.

The integration of career education and English asks more of teachers of English than that they blend activities already in the English curriculum with career education's interest in the development of utilitarian linguistic skills. Career education is based in part upon the belief that English classes and other subject areas take on a role historically handled by the home. Young people today have little opportunity to know very much about their father's, mother's, uncle's, aunt's, neighbor's, or anyone else's work. Career education as it occurs in the English class proposes that something be done for the young people who know only that their father or mother goes down to the plant, goes to the office, or punches a clock. Integrating career education and English in most high schools, junior high schools, and elementary schools entails this new dimension, and it is fair to call this new dimension an opportunity rather than a threat. As a part of the study of business letters or as a part of almost any other study at almost any other grade level, suppose that contact with the working world occurred in one or more of the following ways.

1. Three students spend a day with someone who spends a considerable amount of time answering, rerouting, or in other ways responding to letters.

2. Three students who have a fair grasp of what it is like to be a letter answerer write a page or more of dialogue between a letter answerer and his or her boss, or between a letter answerer and a customer, or between a letter answerer and his or her spouse—or all three if rhetoric is of interest at the time.

3. A letter answerer tells the class or a few class members about the varying abilities, personalities, levels of excellence, and career goals of his or her fellow letter answerers.

4. A letter answerer's typist talks to the class about his or her appreciation of linguistic clarity, consistency, and accuracy.

5. A panel of business managers and civic leaders talk candidly about receiving and writing business letters.

Occurrences such as these would also add excitement to many classrooms in which day after day teachers talk and students sit. Occurrences such as these would provide ways to study semantics, rhetoric, or dialectology involving students' active participation.

There are other ways that students of all ages can make contact with people in careers of their interest and learn language skills at the same time. One or two teachers can locate and request patient cooperation from business people, government employees, and other skilled laborers. For example, nurses, carpenters, teachers, county clerks, department store clerks, personnel officers, and more are willing to write or speak seriously about their work if students and teachers listen and ask significant questions. After an initial letter of introduction or after a classroom-based interview, students and community workers could pair up, writing to one another three or four times in a serious attempt to exchange ideas and to discuss fears and joys associated with the many careers in a community. Language arts instruction can reach out into the community, to its realities, to its lifestyles, and at the same time improve the teaching of skills and the study of language.

Not all blends of career education and English are obvious. Creative drama has the power to help students and teachers investigate and dramatically experience human relationships—power struggles—between workers in society. Suppose that in the imagined absence of a few students, a class agreed to allow the teacher to toss the absent students' work in the wastepaper basket and in other ways treat the students with indifference for a period of time. All but the excluded students would be assigned the task of close observation, watching for signs of frustration, anger, arrogance, or withdrawal. The game should be repeated once at least before similar imaginary situations are explained briefly and experienced through improvisation and discussion. Creative drama students who have seen and felt the emotions inherent in the movement either of the will of the majority or the weight of an unexplained policy against an individual might enjoy the proposition, "Language and all other communicative media are vehicles of social action and are not merely modes of expressing one's self." In this way, experiences in creative drama and the study of the functions and feelings of words are integrated through English and career education. Once again rhetoric finds its way into the integration of career education and English. The depth of understanding is dependent only upon the grade level, the teacher, and the atmosphere in the classroom.

Teachers of English who can visualize the study of business letters, language, and creative drama in these and other ways will not have too much trouble bringing literature, film, and creative writing into the picture. Before considering examples of ways to integrate the teaching of literature and career education, some commonly known words of caution are in order, for they are too easily forgotten under the influence of attempts to tie aesthetic experiences to the human condition, to social problems, and to career education. First, neither the relevance of literature nor the relevance of any single piece of literature is known, for literature is timeless and can be reinterpreted again and again, year after year, in the light of some new brand of literary criticism or in light of some unexpected social, political, aesthetic, or personal event. *Macbeth, The Rainbow, The Ordeal of Running Standing, The Jungle, Plain Speaking, Maiden,* and *The Canterbury Tales* are not accounts of people choosing careers wisely or foolishly. Unfortunately, some day, somewhere, some teacher is going to ask his or her class whether or not Macbeth had the job skills to be a king. A second caution about the use of literature has to do with students' personal grasp of the literature they have read. If students understand a piece fully on their own, then and then only do the applications of the piece to life situations make sense. *Giants in the Earth* is about farming, one might say, but there are few students these days who both read *Giants in the Earth* well and understand enough about farming to ask the relevance of *Giants in the Earth* to the art of making farming a career.

We might remind ourselves, finally, that literary experiences and pieces of literature themselves are cherished in part because they are the property and possessions of individuals to be used as they see fit. Not too long ago, I used my memory of *The Rainbow* in order to understand a woman with whom I spent but one brief evening. Had my teacher taught me that *The Rainbow* was a tool useful in psychoanalysis I would not have had a literary experience, and *The Rainbow* would not have been taught as literature but rather as psychology, sociology, anthropology, or pornography. These cautions—that the relevance of literature is not known and that the application of literature must follow a fully comprehensive and personal reading—need not polarize thoughts on the matter into two camps—one where literature is thought to be sacred, the other where literature is thought to be useless unless it helps people solve economic problems.

Both career education and the teaching of literature have interests in people's attitudes toward work, toward particular careers, and toward career development. In *The Jungle* by Upton Sinclair, Jurgis only occasionally makes aesthetic, moral, or social judgments about the rise of people in Packingtown. Jurgis's concern is for his family's well-being and for his own physical survival. It is Upton Sinclair, writing in the third person, who pictures the moral, social, and aesthetic climates in which Jurgis moves, more or less unaware of anything beyond his family and himself. Teachers of English and students will no doubt be interested further in Sinclair's lengthy exposition of socialist principles, in Sinclair's use of features of the novel's setting to build sympathy for a less than glorious tragic hero, in the rapid disintegration of the Lithuanian traditions, and in the psychological ways each character handled deprivation, alienation, and starvation.

Although these and other aspects of *The Jungle* deserve discussion and should not be given only superficial treatment, one or more of the following classroom activities would facilitate the integration of the teaching of literature and career education. Suppose that prior to students' reading of *The Jungle*, the teacher read, analyzed, or simply summarized Whitman's "I Hear America Singing," Langston Hughes's "A Dream Deferred," Wordsworth's "London," or O'Neill's *The Hairy Ape*. Students could report stories told by parents, grandparents, uncles, and aunts about work experiences, about exploitation of the poor, or about the ugliness of the city. Prior to student reading, parts of *The Jungle* could be read aloud and briefly discussed. Community environments similar in some way—physically, aesthetically, or psychologically—to the setting apparent in the parts of the book already read to the students might be identified and described. Short stories, or only the beginnings of short stories, could be written in response to selected passages from *The Jungle* and in response to selected community environments. Students could use cameras to gather still images of the working conditions in the community. Labor union members can be invited to talk to a few students or to a large group of students. During the reading of the novel, newspaper articles and televised news accounts will undoubtedly relate to the many parts of *The Jungle*.

In these activities and in others, the relevance of literature to career education is seen—without asking such questions as, "Did Jurgis like his job?" or "Can a man be happy even if he has a job he doesn't like?" Although teachers must listen when students ask these kinds of questions, the two cautions studied earlier must be remembered. The relevance of literature is not yet known, and the application of literature must follow a fully comprehensive and personal reading—a reading fostered by classroom activities that reach out into the community, to its people, and to its realities. Literature cannot be read in a vacuum, at least not by young people.

Career education asks no more than the use of community resources to enhance the teaching of language arts skills, no more than the teaching of skills in such a way that the teaching of skills becomes secondary to the study of language and composition, and no more than the recognition of literature's power to address the multiple relationships between work and the human condition.

Learning about Work: A Study of Contemporary Fiction for Children

Patricia Read Russell
Stephen F. Austin State University

Emphasizing the importance of early career awareness and exposure to the world of work, this author describes the variety of recent children's literature that can serve a K-3 language arts teacher in helping young children explore work values and attitudes. An excellent bibliography is included.

Learning about work, its nature and its rewards, is essential in our society. Recently, however, the public has voiced concern that young Americans are not learning this basic lesson. Educational administrators and teachers are responding to the problem by developing career education programs that focus in part on developing positive work attitudes and an understanding of the nature of work in the next generation of workers.

Career education is very important in preschool and in the K-3 grades, since many attitudes become fixed at this time. Yet too little is known about the attitudes toward work and notions about the nature of work that modern writers of children's fiction are presenting to their audiences. My study of 255 storybooks with copyright dates of 1970 and later shows that two out of every three books ignore work entirely, but that the writers who do treat work as a concept (the word itself is rarely used) display positive attitudes toward it. Work allows fictional characters to help themselves and others, to express themselves creatively, to gain recognition from peers and authority figures, and to serve their communities. Thus, a creative teacher can use good stories, the traditional carriers of values in our culture, to implement career education in the early grades.

In fiction, however, information on work and work values, if present at all, will be subordinated to plot and character development. Since these are stories, not tracts, the teacher may need to emphasize the ideas about the purposes and rewards of work that are inherent in the story. The teacher should be aware that one writer may stress persistence as a quality needed to achieve a work goal, while another may show the need to give up unrealistic goals. One may show work as necessary for family survival; another may show it as defining manhood. Writers for young children present a wide variety of perspectives on work, and the suggested reading list at the end of this article may help the teacher find a story appropriate to the concept of work that he or she wishes the students to explore.

Storybooks of the seventies often show the young child that work is something done by someone else. This is not surprising since child labor is not tolerated in our culture. Indeed, children are a short-term economic liability to a family, not an asset. So work is done by others, particularly by adult males—the fathers, older brothers, and other men of the community. Adult females are usually shown to work only if no adult male in the family does so. In these stories, the child character remains ignorant of the nature of the work done and rarely sees the worker on the job. Nor do the stories stress the rewards of work, although a paycheck may be mentioned. In John Steptoe's *Train Ride*, Charlie tells his friends about his older brother, who works at Chock Full o' Nuts on 42nd Street in New York City. Charlie and his pals, who are urban children, have no work to do on a hot summer day. Sometimes children see workers briefly, as Marvin sees the man fixing the pipes beneath the street in *Marvin's Manhole*, by Winifred Rosen, or as Sally sees the grocery store manager in *Messy Sally*, by Gladys Yessayan Cretan. If a mother works, as in Lucille Clifton's book *Everett Anderson's Friend*, the writer rarely specifies her profession but puts emphasis on the difficulties her child faces because Mom is not at home or on her tiredness at the end of the day. The importance of the personal satisfaction she gets from her profession is not shown.

If the child character is under eight, his or her tasks are done at home. The child's work takes on greatest significance when the work of each member is needed for family survival. Since the work of children is not essential in modern urban or suburban middle class life, the stories usually take place in settings remote in either space or time. The setting is usually rural. Mary, in Ann Blades's *Mary of Mile 18*, has to work hard, as does everyone, to make a success of an Alaskan homestead. Even animals must earn their food. Mary's puppy must earn his keep as a watchdog before her father will allow the dog to stay. However, working together can be fun for a family and for an audience. In *McBroom, the Rainmaker*, Sid Fleischman presents a tall-tale view of a family

good one is *Shawn's Red Bike*, by Petronella Breinburg. Instead, the goal is to win a contest. In Ellen Raskin's *Franklin Stein*, lonely Franklin makes a pet monster, which wins "most original pet." Because of his work for the contest, Franklin wins as a friend a girl who also likes to make things. Making something can be a matter of necessity, as in Tomie de Paola's *Charlie Needs a Cloak*. In this book and in Peter Cohen's extraordinary *Authorized Autumn Charts of the Upper Red River Canoe Country*, the authors stress methods, systems, and persistence as ways of overcoming obstacles to success. Characters strive to gain recognition from an audience and, sometimes, to earn money when they stage dramatic performances. The writers emphasize planning, organization, cooperation and the need for rehearsal. When Christina Katerina wants to dance in her own recital, in *Christina Katerina and the First Annual Grand Ballet*, by Patricia Lee Gauch, she has to convince her parents to let her use the newly redecorated basement, draft her friends as dancers and stagehands, make costumes, conduct rehearsals, and, finally, send the curtain-boy on an errand to keep him from ruining the show. These stories show that work does not always go smoothly, and they introduce the reader to such concepts as making mistakes, acknowledging failures, working around people who cannot do their jobs, and abandoning projects too difficult for the available talent.

Stories with adult protagonists usually deal with the larger concerns of community and country. Current fiction emphasizes working for a better environment and for good government. *Henry Bear's Park*, by David McPhail, presents a young protagonist who takes over the care of a park and turns it into a community showplace. Elisa Trimby's *Mr. Plum's Paradise* is similar. In this tale the effort of one gardener to create a spot of beauty in a decayed neighborhood is the catalyst for a community garden in which the whole neighborhood participates. In other stories, like N. M. Bodecker's *The Mushroom Center Disaster*, the initial effort of one character saves a community from ecological or economic disaster. The work of a single government leader can generate cooperative community effort, as it does in Arnold Lobel's *On the Day Peter Stuyvesant Sailed into Town*. But individuals may have to shoulder the responsibility of telling the leaders of government the truth. Both *The Seventh Mandarin*, by Jane Yolen, and *The King's Fountain*, by Lloyd Alexander, stress the point that people suffer if the ruler is unaware of their problems, and in each case a single man summons the courage to inform the king of the harm his actions can cause his people.

Contemporary fiction for young people not only shows what work is and who may benefit from it, it also presents many attitudes toward work that the teacher can use to reinforce positive behaviors and to question negative ones. Generally, those writers who deal with work in their stories show respect for hard work and for doing a job well, while they criticize laziness, leaving jobs unfinished, and exploiting others. John Steptoe's *Birthday* shows black men and women working hard for their people, especially their children, as they establish a new community where, hopefully, there will be no prejudice. Stories like *Girls Can Be Anything*, by Norma Klein, in which children fantasize about what they might become as adults, encourage ambition in readers. Mr. and Mrs. Abbott, in the Adrienne Adams's *The Easter Egg Artist*, urge their son to experiment with many forms of artistic endeavor to find his own style of working. In some stories, work defines adulthood. In Dorothy Parker's *Liam's Catch*, ten-year-old Liam earns praise from the local Irish squire for being "an efficient man" on the fish-spotting tower. On the other hand, laziness can bring diseaser, as it nearly does in *Wild Robin*, by Susan Jeffers, and *Bubba and Babba*, by Maria Polushkin, both retold folktales. Exploiting others leads to humbling and learning experiences for the exploiters in Lloyd Alexander's *The Four Donkeys* and Diane Massie's *Dazzle*. In Frank Asch's *Good Lemonade*, Hank learns that no amount of advertising is a substitute for a good product. Stories for young children even deal with the need for retraining and with mid-career shifts. *Farmer Hoo and the Baboons*, by Ida Chittum, shows the unhappiness of a man who is obsessed with work to the exclusion of fun and then has him learn about play.

Good work by many people is essential to our society. Teachers of the early grades who want their students to understand good work and the rewards it can bring can find current fiction to help them. The pages that follow contain a classified list of some of the books available. In these stories readers and listeners will find characters who learn about the value of work at home and in the world outside. They will find workers who help themselves and others, who work for money or for the fun of it or both. They will find people who care for the very young, for the very old, for the sick. They will meet a boy who makes monsters, witches who bake prize-winning cakes, and a girl who finishes a successful dance recital with the declaration that she's going out for baseball next. Some writers for young children still present the theme that good work is a source of profound satisfaction to human beings. And they tell good stories, too.

Bibliography

Mention of Adult Workers

Clifton, Lucille. *Everett Anderson's Friend.* New York: Holt, Reinhart & Winston, 1976.

Cretan, Gladys Yessayan. *Messy Sally.* Illus. Pat Grant Porter. New York: Lothrop, Lee & Shepard, 1972.

Fraser, Kathleen, and Levy, Miriam F. *Adam's World: San Francisco.* Illus. Helen D. Hipshman. Chicago: Albert Whitman, 1971.

Rosen, Winifred (Casey). *Marvin's Manhole.* Illus. Rosemary Wells. New York: Dial, 1970.

Steptoe, John. *Train Ride.* New York: Harper & Row, 1971.

Farm Work for Family Survival

Adoff, Arnold. *Man Da La.* Illus. Emily McCully. New York: Harper & Row, 1971.

Blades, Ann. *Mary of Mile 18.* Plattsburgh, N.Y.: Tundra Books, 1971.

Fleishman, Albert Sidney. *McBroom, the Rainmaker.* Illus. Kurt Werth. New York: Grosset & Dunlap, 1973.

Hoban, Russell. *Emmet Otter's Jug-Band Christmas.* Illus. Lillian Hoban. New York: Parents Magazine Press, 1971.

Caring for Other Family Members

Adoff, Arnold. *Black Is Brown Is Tan.* Illus. Emily McCully. New York: Harper & Row, 1973.

Gackenbach, Dick. *Hattie Be Quiet, Hattie Be Good.* New York: Harper & Row, 1977.

Jeschke, Susan. *Firerose.* New York: Holt, Reinhart & Winston, 1974.

Lexau, Joan. *Emily and the Klunky Baby and the Next Door Dog.* Illus. Martha Alexander. New York: Dial, 1972.

Paustovsky, Konstantin. *The Magic Ringlet.* Illus. Leonard Weisgard. Reading, Mass.: Addison-Wesley, 1971.

Rayner, Mary. *Mr. and Mrs. Pig's Evening Out.* New York: Atheneum, 1976.

Titus, Eve. *Anatole and the Toyshop.* Illus. Paul Galdone. New York: McGraw-Hill, 1970.

Watson, Pauline. *A Surprise for Mother.* Illus. Joanne Scribner. Englewood Cliffs, N.J.: Prentice-Hall, 1976.

Zolotow, Charlotte. *William's Doll.* Illus. William Pene du Bois. New York: Harper & Row, 1972.

Caring for Pets and Other Animals

Baylor, Byrd. *Hawk, I'm Your Brother.* Illus. Peter Parnall. New York: Scribner's, 1976.

Carley, Wayne. *Puppy Love.* Illus. Erica Merkling. Champaign, Ill. Garrard, 1971.

Parker, Nancy Winslow. *Love from Uncle Clyde.* New York: Dodd, Mead, 1977.

Sendak, Maurice, and Margolis, Matthew. *Some Swell Pup; or, Are You Sure You Want a Dog.* New York: Farrar, Straus & Giroux, 1976.

Skorpen, Liesel Moak. *Bird.* Illus. Joan Sandin. New York: Harper & Row, 1976.

—————. *Michael.* Illus. Joan Sandin. New York: Harper & Row, 1975.

Smith, Kay. *Parakeets and Peach Pies.* Illus. Jose Aruego. New York: Parents Magazine Press, 1970.

Vigna, Judith. *Couldn't We Have a Turtle Instead.* Chicago: Albert Whitman, 1975.

Wondriska, William. *The Stop.* New York: Holt, Rinehart & Winston, 1972.

Aiding Friends and Other Non-Family Persons

Aardema, Verna. *Who's in Rabbits' House?* Illus. Leo Dillon and Diane Dillon. New York: Dial, 1977.

Delton, Judy. *Two Good Friends.* Illus. Giulio Maestro. New York: Crown, 1974.

du Bois, William Pene. *Bear Circus.* New York: Viking, 1971.

Ets, Marie Hall. *Elephant in a Well.* New York: Viking, 1972.

Harrison, David Lee. *The Book of Giant Stories.* Illus. Philippe Fix. New York: American Heritage, 1972.

Horwitz, Elinor Lander. *The Strange Story of the Frog Who Became a Prince.* Illus. John Heinly. New York: Delacorte, 1971.

Krahn, Fernando. *A Flying Saucer Full of Spaghetti.* New York: Dutton, 1970.

Peet, Bill. *Cyrus, the Unsinkable Sea Serpent.* Boston: Houghton Mifflin, 1975.

Piers, Helen. *Snail and Caterpillar.* Illus. Pauline Baynes. New York: American Heritage, 1972.

Raskin, Ellen. *Moose, Goose and Little Nobody.* New York: Parents Magazine Press, 1974.

Steig, William. *Amos and Boris.* New York: Farrar, Straus & Giroux, 1971.

—————. *Farmer Palmer's Wagon Ride.* New York: Farrar, Straus & Giroux, 1974.

Yolen, Jane. *The Bird of Time.* Illus. Mercer Mayer. New York: T. Y. Crowell, 1971.

Work for the Community

Alexander, Lloyd. *The King's Fountain.* New York: Dutton, 1971.

Bodecker, N. M. *The Mushroom Center Disaster.* Illus Erik Blegvad. New York: Atheneum, 1976.

Kraus, Robert. *Pinchpenny Mouse.* Illus. Robert Byrd. New York: Windmill Books (Dutton), 1974.

Lobel, Arnold. *On the Day Peter Stuyvesant Sailed into Town.* New York: Harper & Row, 1971.

E. Louise Patten Library

Diedmont Colleae

McPhail, David. *Henry Bear's Park.* Boston: Little, Brown, 1976.

Trimby, Elisa. *Mr. Plum's Paradise.* New York: Lothrop, Lee & Shepard, 1977.

Yolen, Jane. *The Seeing Stick.* Illus. Mel Furukawa. New York: T. Y. Crowell, 1978.

————. *The Seventh Mandarin.* New York: Seabury, 1970.

Creating Dramatic Performances and Other Projects

Anglund, Joan Walsh. *The Cowboy's Christmas.* New York: Atheneum, 1972.

Bach, Alice. *The Most Delicious Camping Trip Ever.* New York: Harper & Row, 1976.

Binzen, Bill. *Alfred Goes Flying.* Garden City, N.Y.: Doubleday, 1976.

Blood, Charles L., and Link, Martin. *The Goat in the Rug.* Illus. Nancy Winslow Parker. New York: Parents Magazine Press, 1976.

Breinburg, Petronella. *Shawn's Red Bike.* Illus. Errol Lloyd. New York: T. Y. Crowell, 1976.

Cohen, Peter Zachary. *Authorized Autum Charts of the Upper Red River Canoe Country.* Illus. Tomie de Paola. New York: Atheneum, 1972.

de Paola, Tomie. *Charlie Needs a Cloak.* Englewood Cliffs, N.J.: Prentice-Hall, 1973.

Devlin, Wende, and Devlin, Harry. *Old Witch and the Polka Dot Ribbon.* New York: Parents Magazine Press, 1970.

Fassler, Joan. *Howie Helps Himself.* Illus. Joe Fassler. Chicago: Albert Whitman, 1975.

Gauch, Patricia Lee. *Christina Katerina and the First Annual Grand Ballet.* Illus. Doris Burn. New York: Coward, McCann & Geoghegan, 1973.

Hein, Lucille E. *Prayer Gifts for Christmas.* Illus. Carol Nelson. Minneapolis: Augsburg, 1972.

Hutchins, Pat. *Changes, Changes.* New York: Macmillan, 1971.

Keats, Ezra Jack. *Hi Cat!* New York: Macmillan, 1970.

Krahn, Fernando. *April Fools.* New York: Dutton, 1974.

Marshall, James. *Willis.* Boston: Houghton Mifflin, 1974.

Quin-Harken, Janet. *Peter Penny's Dance.* Illus. Anita Lobel. New York: Dial, 1976.

Raskin, Ellen. *Franklin Stein.* New York: Atheneum, 1972.

Turner, Glenette. *Surprise for Mrs. Burns.* Illus. Dan Siculan. Chicago: Albert Whitman, 1971.

Importance of Hard Work and Work Attitudes

Alexander, Lloyd. *The Four Donkeys.* Illus. Lester Abrams. New York: Holt, Rinehart & Winston, 1972.

Asch, Frank. *Good Lemonade.* New York: Franklin Watts, 1976.

Chittum, Ida. *Farmer Hoo and the Baboons.* Illus. Glen Rounds. New York: Delacorte, 1971.

Friedman, Aileen. *The Castles of Two Brothers.* Illus. Steven Kellogg. New York: Holt, Rinehart & Winston, 1972.

Jeffers, Susan. *Wild Robin.* New York: Dutton, 1976.

Kellogg, Steven. *The Mystery of the Missing Red Mitten.* New York: Dial, 1974.

Massie, Diane Redfield. *Dazzle.* New York: Parents Magazine Press, 1969.

Ness, Evaline. *Do You Have the Time, Lydia?* New York: Dutton, 1971.

Parker, Dorothy D. *Liam's Catch.* New York: Viking, 1972.

Polushkin, Maria. *Bubba and Babba.* Illus. Diane de Groat. New York: Crown, 1976.

Ryan, Cheli Duran. *Hildilid's Night.* Illus. Arnold Lobel. New York: Macmillan, 1971.

Steptoe, John. *Birthday.* New York: Holt, Rinehart & Winston, 1972.

Williamson, Jane. *The Trouble with Alaric.* New York: Farrar, Straus & Giroux, 1975.

Career Goals and Problems During Careers

Adams, Adrienne. *The Easter Egg Artists.* New York: Scribner's, 1976.

Freeman, Don. *Bearymore.* New York: Viking, 1976.

Klein, Norma. *Girls Can Be Anything.* Illus. Roy Doty. New York: Dutton, 1973.

Reavin, Sam. *Hurray for Captain Jane.* Illus. Emily Arnold McCully. New York: Parents Magazine Press, 1971.

Stevenson, James. *The Bear Who Had No Place to Go.* New York: Harper & Row, 1972.

Tresselt, Alvin. *Bonnie Bess, the Weathervane Horse.* Illus. Erik Blegvad. New York: Parents Magazine Press, 1970.

Whitney, Alma Marshak. *Just Awful.* Illus. Lillian Hoban. Reading, Mass.: Addison-Wesley, 1971.

Young, Miriam. *If I Flew a Plane.* Illus. Robert Quackenbush. New York: Lothrop, Lee & Shepard, 1970.

English and Career Education:
A Re-vision of Resources

James S. Davis and Roger Nall
Grant Wood Area Education Agency,
Cedar Rapids, Iowa

These authors offer an approach to career education in the
English classroom that is based upon the concept of individual
actualization. Because this broad concept includes four basic
components—work, leisure, use of resources, and development of
the self—the authors contend that it is a more appropriate model
than those which focus on more narrow goals.

Career education has often been interpreted as either a threat to
the humanistic aspects of English or as a rationale for a vocational
language skills curriculum. Neither interpretation is viable. English
teachers, teacher educators, and curriculum leaders need a concept
of career education capable of integrating many positive things
already being done in English classes and of encompassing needed
additions.

An emphasis on job clusters, provision for awareness of occupational choices, and the goal of developing entry level job skills
place a narrowly perceived world of work foremost in conventional career education. As a result, students are frequently expected to learn from vacuous materials for a tenuous future.
A more appropriate concept for the English curriculum is individual actualization, which relates work, leisure, the use of resources,
and development of the self.

Certainly the English curriculum must contribute to the development of language abilities, including those that are overtly
work-related. More is involved, however, than presenting an end-
less progression of application forms; the technical report or con-

This article was originally published in *English Education*, vol. 10 (December 1978), pp. 96–101. Copyright © 1978 by the National Council of
Teachers of English. Reprinted by permission of the authors and publisher.

cise memorandum may be more important than the business letter. We can assert, with some confidence, that good communication is essential to success in the business world, but then comes the task of teaching from our own assertion. Fostering good communication involves more than efforts to eradicate mechanical blemishes. It means teaching organization, brevity, the ability to summarize explicitly and to communicate appropriately to an intended audience. It may mean giving students a sense of how and why communication becomes progressively distilled as it advances through a corporate structure. It probably depends, in part, on developing a delight in producing and receiving well-written communications. And perhaps, even as we endeavor to develop their abilities to communicate, students deserve to know that employers may rank that ability lower than the willingness to work hard, the ability to make judgments, and the ability to work with other people. And, in terms of our assertion, we still must deal with a larger issue, the defining of "success."

The English curriculum is an ideal arena for the consideration of many issues in career education, including the nature of work and its effects on people. Work is a component as well as a significant determiner of lifestyles. If students have the need to develop entry level skills in chosen occupations, they also have the need to base career choices on a knowledge of the relationship between work and lifestyle, with the awareness that an age of change and mobility does allow alternatives. Bolles's *What Color Is Your*

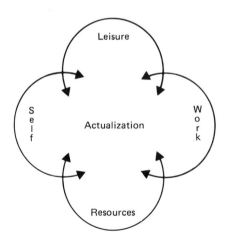

Parachute?, a manual for the mid-life career changer, includes numerous activities which can make students and teachers alike aware of the many options, what and where, in choosing a career. It underscores the benefits of making lifestyle decisions, considering a career as one component. As the corporate domain faces more employees who refuse to sacrifice their families for promotions or transfers, alternative interpretations of work, career, and especially of roles in life become evident.

Today, most work is not only, nor even predominantly, task dependent. It is relationship dependent. Conventional career education presents all work as having dignity and importance; in reality, some work is thoroughly undesirable and demeaning, and all work is distasteful some of the time. People have dignity and worth; they give work its value. They also need satisfaction from it. Studs Terkel's *Working* portrays many individual workers powerfully expressing their feelings about work and about their lives. The vignettes are excellent for use with students and with teachers.

Students also need to develop insight into the human relationships inherent in work situations and the ways they are affected by different perceptions. In one survey ("Appreciation Comes First," Earl Nightingale Program, Chicago: Nightingale-Conant Corporation, 1948) supervisors and employees were asked to rank the factors contributing to employee morale. Employees indicated that they prized full appreciation of work done, feeling "in on things," and sympathetic help with their personal problems. Supervisors thought employee morale was attributable to wages, job security, and promotions. Indeed, they rated least significant the three items employees ranked most significant. In "My Turn: Going My Way" (*Newsweek*, September 22, 1975, p. 17) Martin Krovetz presents a concise example of a developing career and its effect on lifestyle, relationships with family and friends, and self-perception. That Krovetz is in education only makes his statement more readily usable with teachers and prospective teachers. One effective approach to career education inservice is to involve teachers in an analysis of their own career choice and its development and in sharing feelings about their own work.

Work and work-related relationships may significantly affect a person's time off the job. Traditionally categorized as leisure, such time may be devoted solely to recreational activities. However, leisure can provide an avenue for individual renewal, a means of providing balance and proportion to the dimensions of life. It is crucial, necessary, even with fulfilling work. Leisure can provide opportunities to try new things, to engage in new behaviors. It may allow the freedom to succeed or fail in personally chosen endeavors, providing low risk, low threat, experimental situations. It can sustain individual aspirations for which the timing is not yet right.

Utilization of resources has been one of the more limited aspects of individual actualization. Traditionally it has been oriented largely to the use of print materials, limiting the individual's perception of available human resources, organizational resources, and even of the self as a resource. By asking, "What help is available in any area, at any time in my life?" individuals can learn to choose what resources they need to utilize as well as when, where, and how to do so. Resources are not to be drawn upon only to solve problems, but can be used to enhance even the most rewarding areas of our lives. The wide range of resources available to us must be perceived as potential contributors to growth and self-worth. Exciting programs throughout the country, such as those resulting in the *Foxfire* publications and others like them, involve students with people outside the schools, with human resources, and often do so in relation to work or to productive leisure activities. They certainly offer exposure to lifestyles different from the students' own.

Developing self-awareness is a major component of career education if actualization is to be the focus. Realistic self-awareness means coming to terms with self, not accepting limitations imposed by others. Bob Samples's *Opening: A Primer on Self-Actualization* offers valuable information for both students and teachers in pursuing and developing self-understanding. It supports the intrinsic, accepting, developing self, capable of lasting self-esteem and of regard for others. The teacher who desires to help students develop such a self-concept, and who sees it as the unifying component in an English/career education model, must be concerned with providing a preponderance of successes rather than failures, with deleting putdowns from the learning environment, and with allowing a maximum of risk taking. The same characteristics should be evident in efforts to educate English teachers about career education.

This concept of career education can be integrated into English and English teacher preparation through activity-oriented learning. One activity method includes the following stages: (1) *briefing*, in which interest is generated, expectations are created, and the stage is set for further investigation and interaction; (2) *activity*, following through with a procedure, usually providing individual pacing and reasonable time frames; (3) *debriefing*, a time for contemplation and sharing and for the articulation of discoveries, personal implications, and individually formulated goals or action commitments. Voluntary participation in open sharing must be protected in the debriefing stage, but the teacher must plan for all three stages to occur.

1. Activity: 1-2 class periods.

    Briefing. Read "My Turn: Going My Way," by Martin L. Krovetz, in *Newsweek* (September 22, 1975). Discuss factors which might contribute to "us/them" thinking as treated in the article. (Some material from Hayakawa's *Language in Thought and Action* might be valuable here.)

    Activity. Have participants generate characteristics they associate with various "us/them" dichotomies, such as teachers/students, parents/children, old people/young people, blue collar/white collar, men/women. Participants might investigate, through surveys or interviews, attitudes toward particular dichotomous labels which interest them.

    Debriefing. Share survey or interview findings. Discuss them and the characteristics generated by participants. Role play encounters between individuals who hold the attitudes discovered. Talk about how "us/them" thinking keeps some people separated and other people together. Write a journal only about a personal encounter with "us/them" thinking.

2. Activity: 1 class period.

    Briefing. Have participants generate different definitions of "work" (write them on the board). Discuss them briefly, and ask each participant to write down a definition he/she could accept.

    Activity. Read "An Authentic Work Ethic," *Reader's Digest* (January 1977), and selections from the unit "Poets on Work," *Thematic Units in Teaching English and the Humanities* (NCTE, 1975). Discuss the question, "What is work?"

    Debriefing. Involve the students in shared speculation about what definitions of work and attitudes toward it might be more or less functional in various occupations.

3. Activity: Several class periods.

    Briefing. Have participants identify and describe a person who had a significant effect on them and whom they would like to emulate. Have participants write down what they know/believe of the person in each of the actualization components (work, leisure, use of resources, self-concept). For teachers, focus on a person who influenced them into teaching.

Activity. Through interviews, letters, and contacts with mutual acquaintances, generate additional information to fill out the profile as fully as possible in each area.

Debriefing. Analyze the known areas in relation to initial perceptions, and the implications of unknown areas and information. Engage in a shared search for common elements and differences among the individuals chosen.

There are many opportunities for career education in the English curriculum. Career choices and role expectations can be discussed in relation to many literary characters, female and male. A unit can be based on adolescent novels in which the characters are confronting, among other pressures, career decisions and differing lifestyles. Students are often attuned to adolescent characters facing the expectations of other people.

Mark Twain perceived work as what you do when you would rather be doing something else. Maybe that does not have to be true—of students or teachers.

References

Bolles, Richard N. *What Color Is Your Parachute?* Berkeley: Ten Speed Press, 1974.
> Written for the mid-life career changer, this book is rich in self-perception techniques and in approaches to job selection and acquisition.

Ericksen, Erik. "Need to Re-evaluate? Let's Facilitate." *Career Information Systems of Iowa Newsort*, Vol. 1, No. 1. Des Moines: Iowa Department of Public Instruction, 1975.
> Good article on how teachers, counselors, librarians, and administrators can work together to facilitate the career development process.

Hays, Ellis R. *Interact: Communication Activities for Personal Life Strategies.* San Francisco: International Society for General Semantics, 1974.
> Seventy individual activities to develop greater understanding of self and of communication processes. Number 28, "Self-Disclosure," for example, asks participants to look at the contexts in which they disclose the most and best about themselves.

Occupational Outlook Handbook. U.S. Department of Labor, Bureau of Labor Statistics, U.S. Printing Office, 1976.

Resource book used by counselors but also suggested for student use. Gives descriptions of virtually all jobs in the United States, including salaries and projected employment outlooks.

Rural America Series: Career Guidance, Placement, and Follow-Through Program (K-14) for Rural Schools. Columbus: Center for Vocational Education, Ohio State University, 1977.

Equally appropriate for rural and metropolitan areas, this is excellent resource material for people interested in using group processes and human resources in career education.

Samples, Bob. *Opening: A Primer for Self-Actualization.* Reading, Mass.: Addison-Wesley Publishing Co., 1975.

Excellent material for teachers and students on the need for, and factors involved in the processes of self-actualization in contemporary culture.

Schrank, Jeffrey. *TV Action Book.* Evanston, Ill.: McDougal, Littell & Co., 1974.

The final section deals with the issue of effective public action. It offers students an opportunity to see themselves as resources, as people who can affect others and the institutions around them.

Wigginton, Eliot. *Moments: The Foxfire Experience.* IDEAS. Dayton, Ohio, 1975.

Treats the pedagogy and educational philosophy behind the program which resulted in the *Foxfire* books and magazines. Good material on involving students and teachers with human resources.

III Career Education in the English Classroom

Composition Skills and Career Education

Robert C. Small, Jr.
Virginia Polytechnic Institute and State University

Here is a plan for a writing unit that will provide students with the opportunity to learn and practice a variety of writing skills while simultaneously exploring careers from the inside and outside. Utilizing simulation techniques, students would be involved in sixteen different types of writing in a unit designed to fulfill both career education goals and the standard goals of a composition program.

More and more schools are being asked to revise their programs to include greater emphasis on career education. The pressure is coming from all sides: businessmen who feel that schools do not prepare students well to seek employment, parents who worry that their children will leave school to join the unemployment lines, students who see little relation between much that they have to do in school and the practical necessity of earning a living. Many professional educators, frequently but not exclusively from the vocational education areas, are also energetically advising a shift to career education throughout the school.

English teachers, perhaps more than most high school teachers, have difficulty responding to this call for career education since many feel that what they do in their classes relates more to the noncareer aspects of their students' future lives. The area of written composition skills, however, is in many ways closely related to career education. The English teacher performs a major career education service by preparing students who can write clearly, who can, when they want to, conform to the traditional

This article was originally published in *Classroom Practices in Teaching English, 1975-1976: On Righting Writing*, edited by Ouida H. Clapp, pp. 110-13. Copyright © 1975 by the National Council of Teachers of English. Reprinted by permission of the author and publisher.

rules of spelling and mechanics, and perhaps most important, who are able to deal effectively with the requirements of different types of writing. On the other hand, many of the specific career-oriented writing skills which English teachers are asked to teach do not fit easily into the types of writing with which they have been prepared to deal. Consequently, teachers have often presented the skills involved in writing letters of application and in filling out application forms in isolation from the rest of the program. Aside from some emphasis on mechanical accuracy, such lessons have generally had little connection to the rest of the program and have, in fact, seemed to many English teachers to be more appropriately a part of some other subject such as distributive education.

English teachers, usually at the request of the guidance department (and rather unwillingly), have occasionally assigned their students a report on some topic such as "My Future Occupation" and tried to use the assignment as a means of teaching research skills. Lifted in large part from career pamphlets and encyclopedias, such reports have usually been less than successful, either from the career or from the English point of view. In addition to being tedious and irrelevant, such reports have failed because no effort was made to help the student to understand and to feel what being in his or her career choice would be like and to articulate that feeling. Instead, external, largely factual information was all that the student was asked for or given.

It is possible, however, to plan a unit which will provide each student with many opportunities to learn about and practice a variety of writing skills while at the same time explore a career from both the outside (applicant) and the inside (practitioner).

Phase One: Outside

In such a unit, the students would begin in the traditional manner by examining factual information about a selected career and summarizing those facts in a brief presentation, using the skills of outlining and summarizing. Since it is not a research report, there would be no pretense that the result is anything but a condensation of one or more sources. From this summary, the students would then write a list of the characteristics that they have which suit them for that career. At the same time, they would examine want ads or similar materials appropriate to this career and obtain the names and addresses of businesses, agencies, and institutions which employ people in that occupation. They would choose one and write a letter requesting information about work possibilities. They would also ask for copies of job applications, descriptions of application procedures, and so on. When such materials have been obtained, the students would go through the formal application procedures for employment in that career, including possibly a simulated submission to whatever certification processes or examinations may be used in the field.

Phase Two: Inside

Up to this point, the unit would resemble many efforts by English teachers to create simulated situations for the writing of job applications, and it is at this point that most units conclude. Unfortunately, however, such a unit concentrates only on the externals of the career under consideration, and the writing exercises and skills are of a rather low level. If, however, the unit were to be continued by asking the students to pretend that they had, in fact, entered the career under consideration, many additional writing skills could be included. By reading biographies and autobiographies, novels, short stories, and essays by and about persons pursuing a particular career, students would attempt to develop a sense of what it is like to do that kind of work. They might also examine appropriate specialized materials such as journals, manuals, and books.

This second phase would require various types of writing. Students would be expected to interview a person working in that career area and present a written report in the manner of journalistic interviews with well-known people. They would also write a narrative in which they attempted to present the details of the public life of a person in that career. They might also write several short papers from this person's point of view, such as a letter to the editor of a local newspaper reacting to some issue or event, a letter to a colleague, or a report to a superior. The particular skills involved in each type of composition would, of course, be studied as a preliminary to the writing. Descriptive writing would focus on the details of the place of work and would probably require a visit to such a place. Impressionistic writing would involve efforts to capture the various moods of the career and those who pursue it, and character sketches could be written about fellow workers, clients, and others. Again, the particular skills involved in each type of writing would be examined as a part of the writing situation.

Finally, taking the role of an established practitioner of the career, students could prepare a job description to be given to someone considering entering that field. They could also prepare an advertisement for a job opening, using the form appropriate to the career, and develop application materials and procedures. The final step in the unit would consist of reviewing their own applications from Phase One, deciding whether or not to hire themselves on that basis, preparing a report to some appropriate authority explaining the decision, and writing a letter to themselves concerning the decision.

Thus, in such a unit, each student would practice the general skills of composing and also the particular skills involved in the following types of writing:

1. a summary,

2. a list of character elements,

3. a letter asking for information,

4. a job application,

5. a journalistic interview,

6. a narrative,

7. a letter to a newspaper editor,

8. a friendly letter,

9. a report to a superior,

10. a description,

11. an impressionistic piece capturing a mood,

12. several character sketches,

13. a job description,

14. an advertisement,

15. an application form, and

16. a letter to a job applicant.

This composition unit moves students from the outside of a proposed career to the inside, from the position of an uninformed novice to the viewpoint of an expert who makes decisions about job applicants. Because of the emphasis on the inside details of the career, the unit would provide the student with a simulated situation for the practice of many different composing skills, all of which, even the more "creative," would have a meaningful and practical application. Such a unit, then, would meet the challenge of career education and, at the same time, allow for activities appropriate to the objectives of the English composition program.

Language and Career Education for the Middle and Junior High School

Marjorie M. Kaiser
University of Louisville

The author contends that the language aspect of the language arts curriculum provides a rich reservoir of material beyond skills development that can be integrated with career education. The article suggests a variety of exploratory activities for students that will help them realize the interrelationships between language and the world of work while simultaneously reinforcing their curiosity and joy in language itself.

Teachers of language arts throughout the country are illustrating, through locally developed curriculum materials, that they are willing and able to integrate language arts and career education in their classrooms. By and large, these materials focus on the development of language arts skills appropriate to job seeking. These skills include those required in interviewing, completing job applications, and writing letters and reports of various kinds. The development of these language skills is certainly an area in which English teachers can support career education programs, but this emphasis suggests that career education is designed only for students who will seek full-time employment immediately after high school graduation or only for vocational students. Potential college students are interested in careers too, and surely there is much more in a language program for *all* students that could be integrated with career education than just practical skills development.

During the middle or junior high school years in which the major emphasis in career education programs is on exploration—exploration of the world of work, exploration of self, and exploration of specific career clusters—it seems fitting that students explore the language of work as well as the facts of work. In an

This article was originally published in *Language Arts*, vol. 55 (March 1978), pp. 302-7. Copyright © 1978 by the National Council of Teachers of English. Reprinted by permission of the author and publisher.

67

activities-oriented English classroom, students would enjoy and profit from the exploration of language as it is related to work in general and to specific career clusters and individual jobs or professions in particular. Following are some suggested activities that middle or junior high school students could be involved in, not as full units of study, but as mini-units of one or two class periods at a time or as individual student projects. These activities could result in increased student interest in careers, general and specific, and simultaneously in the English language itself.

Work Words

Students at the middle or junior high school level are fascinated with stories about word origins. With even a superficial knowledge of the history of the language—the major periods and influences— which many schools include in their present language curriculum, these students could explore the origins and meanings of words and expressions, such as *work, career, occupation, profession, labor, job, pay, salary, boss, blue collar worker, white collar worker*, and so forth. The discovery that *to pay* traces back to the Latin for *to pacify* or that *salary* meant *salt money* or that *profession* in Middle English referred to a religious declaration or vow or that *job* might have come from the Middle English *jobb*, meaning a *piece*, would enhance students' knowledge of how history brings about language changes and would stimulate their curiosity about other work-related uses of language. Students could examine the development of present-day connotations of and distinctions between such words as *job* and *position, wages* and *salary, work* and *labor*. Good dictionaries, of course, are imperative for this activity, as is some instruction in how to read a dictionary entry if students do not possess this skill.

By examining the following groups of selected words which come from different periods of Old English, students could discover how the language can reveal the occupations of the people who speak it, whether it be a whole nation or a small group of people in a particular modern occupational group:

Group 1—*cliff, east, flood, mast, north, oar, sail, south, steer, moon, sun, star, storm, fish, strand, west, whale, rope, flight, boat*

Group 2—*hunt, deer, fire, tinder, hungry, shoot, flesh*

Group 3—*kettle, cow, calf, sheep, chicken, swine, pig, hut, ox, horse, hood, fat, food, sold, home, tin, father, neighbor, king, door, folk, bath, man, wife, child, bench, corn, crop, roof*

Similar, more lengthly lists could be developed for Middle English, which would show French and Latin influences in the area of government work, the military, law, and medicine as well as other learned professions. And finally, students could compile their own lists of words and expressions created or altered in meaning in Modern English that relate to work or specific kinds of work peculiar to the twentieth century. The television industry, for example, has made a unique contribution to the English vocabulary—*video, telecast, television, TelePrompTer, commercial, video-editor, cue card, anchorman,* and so on.

On-the-Scene Observation

Another activity that would help students realize the relationship between work and language requires an hour or two outside of school. The student could arrange to spend a block of time with a person at work, recording the "work language" of that individual. A cassette tape recorder could be used, or the student could simply take notes while observing the person working. Afterwards, the student could tally the work-related vocabulary peculiar to that particular job or profession. Persons in the community who might agree to such observations include lawyers, law enforcement officers, radio or television personnel, retail business persons, doctors, dentists, veterinarians, judges, restaurant owners or employees, transportation personnel, factory workers, hospital employees, service station mechanics, and others. In situations where the public is involved, the student could note differences in vocabulary and expressions used with co-workers and those used with the public, if such differences exist. Exploring these differences in language for different audiences could help reinforce the concept of language as purposeful communication. Does the restaurant waitress, for example, use the same vocabulary and expressions with the customer and the cook? The doctor with the nurse and the patient? Sharing observations on these differences could lead students to fuller awareness and appreciation of the important part language plays in the world of work.

Career Education Literature

After this firsthand observation, students could examine career education literature—books, pamphlets, folders—available in the school, making lists of vocabulary and expressions that are peculiar to various career clusters or to specific jobs within the clusters. Jobs in the data-processing family, for example, reveal a wide and relatively new and particularized set of words and expressions, even including a meaning of *language* that may be novel to many students. Jobs in the health occupations cluster provide immense lists of vocabulary words, from those associated with nutrition to those used by the physical therapist, the pharmacist, the radiologist, and on and on. Jobs in marine science, transportation, mining, manufacturing, and environmental control will yield their peculiar vocabularies. The variety and extent of these vocabularies could further impress upon students the interrelationships of language and work.

Occupational Titles

Middle or junior high school students know that our language often has more than one word for a given thing or state or act; most can list synonyms for nearly any word a teacher mentions. By the sixth, seventh, or eighth grade, most students are aware that certain words carry certain shades of meaning while others carry other shades. It is possible that they have not yet considered connotation in regard to occupational titles. Nevertheless, if asked, they could list alternate titles for such an occupation as law enforcement officer. No doubt, they would come up with *policeman, cop, copper, fuzz, pig, heat,* and so forth. With such a list, a teacher could ask students to consider the feelings behind the use of such titles. How do they differ? What is the difference between a *psychiatrist* and a *shrink,* a *doctor* and a *pill peddler, music program director* and *disc jockey, garbage collector* and *sanitation engineer, mechanic* and *grease monkey, soldier* and *GI, chef* and *cook, secretary* and *girl Friday, housewife* and *homemaker?* If students consider the conceptions behind alternate titles and look for examples themselves, they will come to appreciate a basic semantic concept—that meanings are in the users of the language, not in the words as such. Literal meanings or denotations, through use, take on positive, negative, or specialized meanings. By examining pairs of occupational titles, such as those previously listed, students could explore the importance of status in job titles as well as move toward a comprehension of the concept of euphemism.

Work Language on Television

Television programming offers students another good source for observing the language of work. As students watch some of their favorite programs, they can note special uses of language as it relates to work. Specific programs which focus on the occupations of the principal characters would be especially useful. Programs on policework abound, as do those on medicine and law and such job areas as truck driving, private detective work, television production, psychology, aviation, and teaching. In many of these programs, the work itself is not the chief focus but merely provides background for human interest stories. Still, any authenticity a serious program claims is due at least in part to the language in the script that lends an air of reality to the drama. In addition to the observation of work language in these programs, students could be observing lifestyles and other areas pertinent to the goals of career education. This observation would require a recognition on the part of the teacher and students that television drama may not always be realistically accurate, and findings need to be compared with information gained from other sources in real life.

In addition to dramatic programs, students interested in sports careers will find a plethora of televised sporting events and interviews with athletes which they can view with an ear toward general sports language and the specialized language of individual sports. Likewise, occupations in music and the dance are featured occasionally and could provide illustrations of the importance of language even in these fields of work. Special documentary programs often focus on the work of archeologists, anthropologists, medical researchers, deep sea divers, scientists of many kinds, political and military figures, and others.

Occupational Naming

Middle or junior high school students are generally curious about the origins of their own names, but they are probably unaware that 20 percent of American surnames derive from occupational titles, going back to the Middle English period. *Smith*, the second most common name in America, *Taylor, Miller, Weaver, Baker,* and *Archer* are obvious examples, but students might enjoy examining other names of English origin which once identified a person's occupation or official position. Such names include the following, among many others.

> *Ambler*—horseman
>
> *Bailey*—bailiff
>
> *Foster*—forester
>
> *Lambert*—lamb herder
>
> *Naylor*—nail maker
>
> *Sawyer*—carpenter
>
> *Turner*—woodworker

Names of other than English origin make up a large portion of the names in the American population. Many of these, too, were originally related to occupations. *Cohen,* for example, the most common Jewish name is this country, is from the Hebrew for priest. *Einstein* meant a builder with stone; *Perlman* and *Perlmutter* were dealers in pearl and mother-of-pearl; *Cantor* was a soloist in the synagogue; while *Lehrer* was a teacher. *Cook* and *Shoemaker* come from the German *Koch* and *Schumacher.* The Spanish name *Calderone* identified a maker of kettles.

Students could investigate the origins of their own names and those of their relatives and neighbors to determine whether they were occupationally oriented. They could also have fun imagining that workers today adopted their names on the basis of their occupations. They could then invent names for people in current occupations they find listed in *The Dictionary of Occupational Titles* and devise a system for sorting out all the teachers, lawyers, salesmen, and engineers from one another. Which names would be most common? What would one call the person whose job it is to shape Hershey chocolate into kisses? Or the person whose job it is to remove rubber particles from the sludge in a rubber factory? How would a person be named whose job title is Mined Land Reclamation Inspector Position Number 00027? Or how would a person be named if his or her title were Feedlot Pest Management Scout Supervisor? And what about a son who assumed the same occupation? Considering whether occupational naming would be desirable at this time in history could make for lively discussion. Such an imaginative excursion into the world of occupational titles would provide fun with language while also familiarizing students with an important reference work in career education.

Occupational Word Making

Students typically enjoy making up new words. They do it naturally from a very early age and continue to do so at least among their peers throughout adolescence. Teenage slang, probably at its peak during the middle and junior high school years, is in fact responsible for a great many pure root creations, semantic change words, and idiomatic compounds which eventually bring new words into the language. Consequently, students are generally fascinated with the word-making process itself. The jargons of various occupations are also responsible for contributing significantly to our language. Students could build lists of words that have been created for new items or processes, or words which have taken on new meanings as a result of use in some occupation or field of industry. They could examine lists provided by the teacher and investigate the principles involved in the making of new words. Some words and compounds which come from occupations and industry and which might interest students today include *leisure suit, meter maid, test drive, crock pot, splashdown, medic, microwave, idiot sheets, computerize, Lip-Quencher, Astroturf, Vista-Vision, Instamatic,* and so forth. Examining daily newspapers and weekly magazines will yield words which are working their way into the language but which may not yet be recorded in dictionaries. Students could examine these words to decide whether their origins are occupational. Perhaps the most enjoyable activity would be for students to dream up a product or process from some area of the world of work and create the language that might derive from it.

Work Language and Literature

Finally, most middle or junior high school literature anthologies contain at least a few selections in which specific occupations or professions are crucial to the plot and/or theme and characterization. Students could read some of these selections, noting uses of language or vocabulary words that are particularized by the kind of work being performed. Nonfiction selections written with the intent to inform as well as entertain may provide the best literary sources, but occasionally fiction, poetry, and drama are appropriate sources as well. After dealing seriously with the language of work in the literary selections, students will probably enjoy looking at the work language of the fictional Walter Mitty as he progresses from one dream to the next, assuming one heroic occupational role after another.

No doubt the teacher can create other learning activities for middle or junior high school students that will help them become aware of the importance of language to work, perhaps even beginning with the language of schoolwork. This awareness of the interrelationships of language and work, a positive in itself, could lead to a broader awareness of the importance of language to nearly every aspect of students' present and future lives while simultaneously creating or sustaining a curiosity and joy in language itself.

Resources

Room-library materials that would be helpful in facilitating the kinds of language exploration proposed here include the following:

1. current newspapers and magazines;
2. desk-sized dictionaries for each student;
3. one unabridged dictionary;
4. several basic language books, including a general overview of the history of the language as well as brief introductions to other aspects of language study (*The Language Book* by Franklin Folsom, *The Tree of Language* by Helene and Charlton Laird, and *The Language of Man* edited by J. F. Littell);
5. other books on word histories (*Dandelions Don't Bite* by Leone Adelson and *What's Behind the Word?* by Harold Longman);
6. *American Surnames* by Elsdon C. Smith;
7. *The American Language* by H. L. Mencken;
8. *Dictionary of Occupational Titles;*
9. pamphlets and other materials on career clusters and specific occupations.

Career Investigation and Planning in the High School English Curriculum

Richard E. Roberts
Arlington Senior High School, Poughkeepsie, New York

This essay outlines an individualized senior elective course emphasizing literature, writing, and research activities. The philosophy and psychology of work undergird each unit, and the units progress from the internal (self-knowledge) to the external (knowledge of specific careers). Suggestions are presented for readings, audiovisual materials, trips, and guest visits, as well as for methods of evaluation in this noncompetitive kind of program.

For the teacher of English who may have been wondering how to fit career education to the language arts program, serious consideration should be given to that branch of career education generally known as "career investigation and planning." While high school literature anthologies have long included thematic units under enticing headings like "Let's Explore Careers!" or "Causes and Careers," somehow in the eyes of the student this is still storybook stuff. In fact, the matter is still being presented in a storybook way: three weeks of exploring careers, then on to "Courageous Decisions," or "Science Fiction and Fantasy." What's really being explored is *literature*, and the aim is to get students to see how literature is related to life and vice versa ("In literature, as in life, we . . ."); thus the matter remains largely academic. The fact is that many high school English programs remain literature oriented, rather than literature grounded.

The pleasant thing about an English course in career investigation and planning is that, while it is sustained by literature, as we'll soon see, it is centered first and foremost in the interests and needs of the student. A broad range of reading, writing, and re-

This article was originally published in the *English Journal*, vol. 66 (November 1977), pp. 49-52. Copyright © 1977 by the National Council of Teachers of English. Reprinted by permission of the author and publisher.

search activities helps students crystallize their thinking about themselves, the world of work, their entry into and place in it. Possibly best offered as a senior elective with no prerequisites other than the students' intuitive desire to learn more about themselves and careers that interest them, the course can utilize *all* of the communications skills commonly associated with the English language arts. The approach, largely individualized, encourages students to see for themselves where they are in their thinking about the world of work, exposing them to a wealth of ideas and experiences designed to bring them along to an enlightened and realistic career decision.

Very few concessions need be made for the so-called slow learner. Most students will perform at a capacity hitherto unimagined by them (or by their teachers) once they realize that what they are doing is of direct benefit to them. Putting it another way, these are things that had better be done well. And so they now apply their vast stores of energy to details that formerly seemed to have no significance. The scrutinizing of a poem for the thoughts hidden between the lines; the careful attention paid to structuring, punctuation, and capitalization in the writing of a business letter; the painstaking research in the school library; even the well-considered oral response to a question like, "Why do you think you might like to work for our company?"—all these skills come into full play here and make sense to all but a few.

If concessions are made, they can be made by way of providing optional assignments at varying levels of difficulty. For those students who are either more capable or more ambitious or both, the opportunity to probe further can be offered. The teacher might, for example, have the entire class read Bill Sands's inspirational autobiography, *My Shadow Ran Fast*, but only a few who appear interested in a corporate career would read the story of the Watsons and IBM in William Rodgers's *Think*. Again, each student might be required to seek out and read a magazine or newspaper profile of some prominent person engaged in the line of work he or she is interested in at the moment, or perhaps to monitor a career tape of someone who works at the job. However, only a few who are either motivated or specially equipped might be asked to prepare and present to the class a photo essay entitled, "A Day in the Life of Harry Wilcox, Architect."

It would be well at this point to inject a word about the broader aims of such a course. By now, it might have occurred to the teacher reading this article that this isn't just a nuts-and-bolts course in career planning. The fact is, the philosophy and psychology of work are given a prominent place throughout all phases of the investigation—mainly through the medium of literature, and specifically by way of selective lists of familiar (and some not so familiar) works grouped at the end of each unit and offered as suggested readings.

Human endeavor has always been a concern of writers, but perhaps the lessons proffered by these talented people of vision have been somewhat lost to us in recent times. How many people have any real commitment to what they do for a living? How many would rather be doing something else if, as they say, they had their way? (It is generally accepted that they don't.) The sad part of it is that these "trapped" people not only believe now, but believed from the very beginning, that they were victims of a system over which they had little or no control. Worse yet, their feelings and attitudes about work are transmitted directly to their children by a curious and misleading set of contradictions.

"Stay in school!" says Dad to his son. "I didn't, and look at me. I'm stuck behind those machines eight hours a day, five days a week, forty-nine weeks a year. And what have I got to show for it? You want to be working like that for the rest of your life, for $220 a week?"

But the youngster has no basis for comparison and only a very limited understanding of the problem. His idea of what his father actually does for a living is vague, since his father talks very little about his work. The old man seems to be doing all right. He's had the same job for as long as the youngster can remember. Dad goes to work every day and brings home a paycheck at the end of the week. With what he makes, and with what Mom and the others bring home, they all live pretty good. The family owns three cars and has a backyard pool. Then there's the bike he got for his birthday, which he helped pay for. They live as well, if not better, than the others in the neighborhood. And they worked for what they got—all of them. "You get what you work for"—that's what Dad always said, wasn't it? And what's wrong with 220 bucks a week? Boy, if he only made that kind of money at the supermarket right now! But that takes time and hard work. The young man knows that. But *it is work* that gets you the things you want out of life, *and not education.* So what's the old man talking about, "Stay in school"?

Actually, what the "old man" was talking about was never said. And if teachers are inclined to doubt that this view of work is firmly rooted in the minds of some of their students, it might be worthwhile to try an experiment.

After a few weeks of your course ask one of your more tired-looking (though attentive) students why he hasn't yet turned in his essay on the theme, "What Is There for Me to Choose From?" He will, in all likelihood, tell you, feeling perfectly justified in his answer, that he hasn't been able to find the time to do it; he goes right to work after school. Possibly, in the way suggested above, this idea of "work" has settled in with him as some sort of canon, at once ennobling and extenuating in its implications—and to the exclusion of any consideration of alternatives that might offer him a better way to mold his future and thereby gratify some deeper instinct within him that has yet to surface. (Ask the same student if he would work if he didn't have to.) Regrettably, there are those who will never gain an understanding of the real values of work and who will be, to a large degree, disenchanted throughout their entire working lives.

It is hoped, then, that by perusing the reflections of thoughtful people as they observe themselves and others at work, the student will gain some valuable insights into the deeper meaning of the work process, and what can and cannot be accomplished by it.

Before leaving this point, it should be noted that the decision as to what is to be read should rest finally with the teacher *and* the student. To this end, readings should be offered only as suggestions and should in no way restrict the choice. No list can be exhaustive, and while readings can be conveniently grouped by theme and are usually available in paperback editions or hardcover anthologies already on school bookshelves, if a student has some particular interest, he or she should be encouraged to pursue it through whatever literature the teacher and student agree on.

As to the matter of audiovisual materials, the teacher need be limited only by the school's budget allotment, the AV facilities in his school, and the demands on time. Currently, there is a burgeoning market for software in the career education field, some of it quite appropriate for a course like this. The best of it would deal with case histories where choices and alternatives are involved. Later on in the course, "how to" films, strips, or sound recordings might be used to advantage. But, oddly enough, the usual success story is most vulnerable to rejection (and often ridicule) by students who are chary of good-intentioned efforts to direct them to the ways of salvation. Curiously, it is only through a taste of disillusionment (such as is sometimes offered by network TV white papers like *The Blue Collar Trap* or *Higher Education: Who Needs It?*) that students are jarred into a fuller awareness of the many real problems confronting them as they prepare to take their places in adult society. Negative views and hard looks at the world do not necessarily produce negative responses. Students most often tend rather quickly to identify the problems depicted and to seize on ways of dealing with them—and that is precisely where intellectual and personal growth begins.

The *opportunities-are-there, world-is-yours, choose-from-these-exciting-new-fields* types of presentations are probably the least effective AV materials for a course of the kind we are talking about here, though it may seem otherwise at first. What should be remembered is that successful career exploration and planning begin at the level of personal discovery. It is here that the growth pattern is established. Glowing pictures of Industry at Work at its many tasks shot-gunned at young people tend to obstruct or at least blur the decision-making process which is at the heart of sound career exploration. Better to say: "What field are you thinking about right now? We may have a filmstrip or cassette that will give you some background and ideas to help you decide whether this might be for you."

For the same reasons, field trips might best be scheduled on an individual basis—except where a class might, let's say, learn about how some leading employer in the community is organized to process job applicants or indoctrinate, train, and advance its employees. This information is valuable to all, whereas what is actually done by the company by way of its business and job classifications is valuable to only a few.

The order of presenting the units in the course will more likely succeed if it is progressive. (See the list of units and readings at the end of this paper.) Effective career planning requires that students assemble and evaluate data along two broad fronts: internal and external. The first two units can be designed to provide students with basic information about themselves (internal) that is revealing and useful in determining how their career interests might best be served in light of their personalities, background, capabilities, needs, and aspirations. The third unit can turn the direction of the search outward, where students can take a look at the field or fields that interest them. It is here that students first begin to translate dreams into realities, often breaking away from puerile or unrealistic career selections. The fourth unit can expose students to the routes and strategies that are most often used to open doors. Unit five can alert them to what they should and should not expect once they are on the job, and unit six can offer them, finally, the opportunity to appraise in retrospect the data they have assembled about and for themselves to the point of gathering the necessary momentum that they will need to carry them forward with a full measure of confidence in the knowledge that they are on the right track to a fuller, more enlightened way of life.

Lastly, it might be well to consider how the teacher is to evaluate student progress in a course of this kind. Career exploration is, by its very nature, a noncompetitive activity. While competition plays a key role in advancing toward a given career goal, one student does not compete with another during the initial stages of searching and planning. Logically, then, grading would seem to have little or no bearing on what students learn or do not learn about themselves and careers that interests them. The test and measure of this comes later. But respecting the need to comply with the more traditional aspects of schooling, the teacher will most likely be expected to record some indications of students' progress.

One suggestion for evaluation that would seem to make sense is to award a standard grade of, say, 95 or A for each assignment turned in and completed in a particular unit, grading down from there for points not fully covered or simply left out. Thus, as is most usual, a report not turned in at all would earn nothing, or a grade of zero. Grade reports could then be based strictly on a simple numerical average over any given period. The theory here is to hold as nearly as possible to an objective grading system, based only on what is or is not turned in, thus anticipating the condition that most usually arises on the job; that is, you derive benefits for the thoroughness of your work—thoroughness being one commonly accepted standard for performance. (Excellence is a measure that is harder to define. While not unknown as a means of evaluating an employee's work, it runs over into a more subjective appraisal of proficiency.)

On the other hand, this is still an English course, albeit functional, and the teacher may wish to evaluate at the level of effective communication, as this pertains to the language arts skills being utilized to complete the report assignments. There is no reason why one couldn't, say, award two grades: one for thoroughness of coverage and the other for correctness of expression if the latter is an important consideration in the evaluation procedure.

Themes and Units: Related Readings

Unit One—Who Am I?

W. H. Auden, "The Unknown Citizen"
Richard Bach, *Jonathan Livingston Seagull*
Willa Cather, "Paul's Case"
Ralph Waldo Emerson, "Self-Reliance"
Hermann Hesse, *Demian*
Bernard Malamud, "A Summer's Reading"
Eugene O'Neill, *Ah, Wilderness!*
Edward Arlington Robinson, "Miniver Cheevy"
J. D. Salinger, *The Catcher in the Rye*
Bill Sands, *My Shadow Ran Fast*

Unit Two—What Do I Want out of Life?

Robert Frost, "Two Tramps in Mud Time"
Sinclair Lewis, "Land"
Arthur Miller, *Death of a Salesman*
Ogden Nash, "Kindly Unhitch That Star, Buddy"
Clifford Odets, "Waiting for Lefty"
Carl Sandburg, "Money"
Studs Terkel, *Working*
Henry David Thoreau, "Life without Principle"
John Updike, *Rabbit, Run*

Unit Three—What Is There for Me to Choose From?

Claude Brown, *Manchild in the Promised Land*
John Galsworthy, "Quality"
Michael Harrington, "The Poverty of the Bowery"
Nat Hentoff, *Jazz Country*
Sinclair Lewis, *Babbit*
Edwin Markham, "The Man with the Hoe"
George Milburn, "A Student in Economics"
Eugene O'Neill, *Beyond the Horizon*
Elmer Rice, *The Adding Machine*
Edward Arlington Robinson, "Cassandra"
William Rodgers, *Think*
Theodore Roethke, "Dolor"
James Thurber, "The Secret Life of Walter Mitty"

Unit Four—How Do I Go About Getting the Job?

Juvenal L. Angel, *Why and How to Prepare an Effective Job Resume*
Richard Nelson Bolles, *What Color Is Your Parachute?*
Sidney Edlund and Mary Edlund, *Pick Your Job—And Land It!*
Glenn L. Gardiner, *How You Can Get the Job You Want*
Richard K. Irish, *Go Hire Yourself an Employer*
Austin Marshall, *How to Find a Job*
Austin Marshall, *How to Get a Better Job*
Dean B. Peskin, *The Art of Job Hunting*
Allan Rood, *Job Strategy*
Sarah Splaver, *Your Career If You're Not Going to College*
Phoebe Taylor, *How to Succeed in the Business of Finding a Job*

Unit Five—What Happens When I Get the Job?

Frederick Lewis Allen, "Horatio Alger, Jr."
Hamlin Garland, "Under the Lion's Paw"
Edgar Lee Masters, "Judge Selah Lively"
Arthur Miller, *All My Sons*
Laurence J. Peter and Raymond Hull, *The Peter Principle* and *The Peter Prescription*
William Saroyan, "Where I Come From People Are Polite"
Upton Sinclair, *The Jungle*
Dennis Smith, *Report from Engine Co. 82*
Irving Stone, *Jack London, Sailor on Horseback*
Mark Twain, "Learning the River"
William Carlos Williams, "In Chains"

Our Vocation to Teach the Vocations: The Integration of Career Education with the Teaching of Literature and Writing

Robert Shenk
United States Air Force Academy

It is our ethical responsibility as teachers to help students explore both the positive and negative aspects of work in the lives of human beings. This exploration can be done through a vast range of excellent literature and imaginative writing, discussion, and simulation activities. The author argues that we can only increase students' aesthetic appreciation of literature by involving them in such activities.

Is it possible to teach literature and writing from the angle of "career education" without destroying the literature, or debasing the writing instruction to a mere matter of technical skill? Such a thing would be possible if our literature contained substantial portraits of various kinds of vocations, and if each one of those portraits made an attempt to delineate the value, meaning, or import of the specific line of work under consideration. As an example of what I mean, consider the following passages from the trilogy *U.S.A.*, in which novelist John Dos Passos attempts to describe the meaning or import of Frank Lloyd Wright's career. Dos Passos begins in this way:

> The son and grandson of preachers, [Wright] became a preacher in blueprints,
>> projecting constructions in the American future instead of the European past.

What did Wright preach?

>> the horizons of his boyhood,
>> a future that is not the rise of a few points in a hundred selected stocks, or an increase in carloadings, or a multiplication of credit in the bank or a rise in the rate on callmoney,
>> but a new clean construction, from the ground up, based on uses and needs . . . .

Naturally, Wright's life was both stormy, and

> full of arrogant projects unaccomplished (How often does the preacher hear his voice echo back hollow from the empty hall, the draftsman watch the dust fuzz over the carefullycontrived plans, the architect see the rolledup blueprints curl yellowing and brittle in the filingcabinet.)

But it was also filled with satisfaction.

> the building that is most completely his is the Imperial Hotel in Tokyo that was one of the few structures to come unharmed through the earthquake of 1923 (the day the cable came telling him that the building had stood saving so many hundreds of lives he writes was one of his happiest days).

And Wright's life was pregnant with meaning. For Wright considered that

> Building a building is building the lives of the workers and dwellers in the building.
> The buildings determine civilization as the cells in the honeycomb the functions of bees.[1]

Clearly, in these short passages, Dos Passos has presented details which suggest something of the real human significance and meaning of Wright's life and profession. Nor is Dos Passos the only novelist to have done such a thing. In fact, writers of all kinds—novelists, poets, dramatists, biographers—have throughout our civilization considered the subjects of labor and vocation, portraying as does Dos Passos the quest for worth, usefulness, and satisfaction in work on the one hand, and the frustration and bitter futility which is often encountered in such a search on the other. Because of this, it is both possible and practical to integrate a genuine humanistic concern about work, vocation, and careers with the teaching of good and even of great literature and with relevant writing assignments. Indeed, I am convinced that we are missing a bet, doing a disservice to our students, and, most important, not realizing the full values and implications of our literature, if we do not develop an eye for these things and begin to speak to them with sensitivity and understanding. But in order to demonstrate this, I should like to make several points, illustrating as I do by reference to specific works of literature and related exercises and writing assignments the kind of approach I am talking about.

First of all, it is simply true that Western literature from its very inception, that is, from Homer himself, has imaged a variety of vocations in their individuality and in their purposeful exercise. It has been often remarked that the *Odyssey* is so accurate in geographic description and maritime detail that Homer must have obtained his facts from some early sea captain, or have been a sailor himself. In any case, his hero Odysseus is first and perhaps foremost a sailor, although certainly also a king, a soldier, and general man of the world. Not only does he know the paths of the seas, but the structure and building of boats—building a boat is his first occupation in the *Odyssey*, and the first adventure he encounters is a shipwreck in which he must use all his knowledge of the sea and his skill to survive. In fact, the universal skill with the hands of Homer's hero, who has also built his own palace and fashioned his bed from a tree trunk, and who has a consummate knowledge both of the construction and the use of his weapons, is of the first importance in understanding Homer's conception of civilization and its basis in skill or cunning of the most practical kind, this in addition to the skill and cunning of ruling. Homer is, of course, but the first of a long line of poets and writers to write of the need for prudence in statecraft, a necessity illustrated not only in Odysseus' own wisdom but in the cleverness of Penelope's weaving of the shroud, and in the prudence and modesty of King Alcinous' daughter, Nausicaa. The same theme is revealed in the lives of more mundane characters, such as the shrewd Eurycleia, Odysseus' nurse, who recognizes her master while washing his legs, but who keeps her head as she does. And there is also Eumaeus, the faithful swineherd, who experiences in his very humble occupation the same hospitality and charity on the one hand, and the craft, strength, and watchfulness on the other, that are found in the palaces of statesmen and rulers. In short, the theme of the necessity for shrewdness or craft in human endeavor is deeply interwoven throughout this seminal text of our literature.

In another cornerstone literary text, craft and occupation are not only prominent subjects, but they provide what is perhaps the pivotal theme. This text, of course, is Chaucer's *The Canterbury Tales*. Like Homer, Chaucer pays closer attention especially in his *Prologue* to the particular details of each person's occupation or craft; the shrewd lawyer, shipman, and reeve are in their own ways comparable to the wily Odysseus, while the yeoman, cook, and even the Wife of Bath in her weaving are noted as being renowned for their practical skill. Chaucer pays special attention to the details of the paraphernalia and dress required of each profession, and it is interesting in this context to dwell in class on the much lessened degree to which modern people can be identified by their trappings and clothes, and upon the question as to whether our own sense of identity suffers as a result. Indeed, thoughtful consideration of the *Prologue* as a whole may suggest that one of the best ways to gain a personal sense of identity is through taking up a particular calling, and this possibility merits very serious consideration in our times, which provide much less in the way of a sense of identity than did the ages of Homer and Chaucer. For not only does an occupation in Chaucer give one identity in the sense of clothing, skills, and special kinds of knowledge, but it also provides a person with something to live up to, or an implied purpose and duty in living. Professional ethics is of course a very prominent modern topic, but in the *Prologue*, the profession itself seems to be a way of being ethical, as if a person can be judged by the degree to which he lives up to his trade. Seen in this light, the description of each pilgrim in the *Prologue* can be the subject of verbal or written comparisons between the ideal and the actual, or between what a pilgrim implicitly agrees to do by being a member of a profession ("profession" here is seen in its sense as a commitment or vow), and what he actually does. Perhaps more readily applicable to modern life are assignments which require students to describe some of their own friends in Chaucer's way—their fellow classmates, for example, who

> find the TV more amusing
> than to do battle with chemistry
> and find that they're losing,

or the corner grocer whose cheating perhaps has prompted a few students to try to outwit him, just as the students in Chaucer's "Reeve's Tale" try to outdo the miller. These examples are just a few illustrations of how the inventiveness of Chaucer's depictions of these professions can stimulate thinking about the issues involved in all occupations, and at the same time develop an appreciation of the achievement of the poet himself.

One might go on describing such themes from the classics of Western literature, and suggest, for example, a number of issues in Shakespeare that can be fruitfully approached with an eye to the meaning of a particular profession, for Shakespeare imaged such professions as ruler and statesman, politician and orator, soldier and leader, courtier and counselor, wife, merchant, player, poet, student and judge, each in its own particular character, purpose, potential for fulfillment, and particular temptations and frustrations. But enough has already been said to establish the fact that work, occupation, and calling are standard and intriguing subjects that have been meaningfully treated in some of the greatest literary works of our culture. I would like to turn now to modern literature and discuss in relation to a variety of modern works the degree to which they, too, can be meaningfully explored in terms of their portraits of work and the professions. Here, just as before, such an approach, far from destroying the literature, will often bring home some of its real value and worth.

It is useful in approaching modern literature to speak directly to the issue of choosing a career, which is so important to students and which is usually very interesting to them as well. Indeed, a whole course or unit can be organized about this concern, and such a unit would ultimately touch on most other important humanistic issues connected with work and careers. We might begin with what is perhaps the most lively and vital portrait of someone finding a calling in all of American literature, and that is, of course, Mark Twain's account of the cub pilot in the first part of his *Life on the Mississippi*. This famous and humorous account is especially attractive to students because of the element of romance in the work, an element that is very important. Students can be led to consider its implications by describing some of their fellows who are all afire to be doctors or lawyers, and then by imagining or depicting what realistic difficulties those students are likely to face, possibly patterning all of this after Twain's account. For even the potential for disillusionment is brought out in the text, in Twain's famous comparison of his initial romantic view of the sunset on the water with what he sees later when he becomes aware of the dangers beneath, and in his further comparison of this disparity with what he thinks a doctor must face, ever looking for disease underneath beauty. This kind of focus on the text itself, along with verbal or written imitations of it, can bring up important considerations concerning the danger of overly romanticizing a particular calling. Yet the requirement to study and describe the character of Bixby the pilot and perhaps compare him with his bumbling apprentice may suggest that there is some truth to the romance after all, in the sense of the personal growth in ability and manhood that is involved in the mastering of a profession.

Much more could be said about Twain's *Life on the Mississippi*, which, although less than sixty pages in length, is a classic of its kind. But of course Twain's work is not alone in portraying the discovery of a stimulating calling. Alex Haley considered the discovery of a very different kind of profession in *Roots*, where he wrote of Chicken George's discovery of his great talent as a game-cocker. And Haley's recent TV account of his own discovery of a vocation through the success of the love letters he ghost-wrote for his naval shipmates now has become very well known. Such accounts as these perhaps need to be set alongside other kinds of experiences and literature to which they can be compared and contrasted—works such as Sir Walter Scott's *Rob Roy*, in which the main character returns to his true vocation in his father's firm after leaving it in quest of adventure, or Morton Thompson's *Not as a Stranger*, in which a man with an obsession to be a doctor goes through the shattering experience of discovering what a doctor is not. However, it may be more appropriate for students to participate imaginatively in literature portraying significant and meaningful careers in progress. By reading and considering works of this kind, students can get a taste of the future implications of present vocational decisions. For example, the issue in Bel Kaufman's *Up the Down Staircase*, as to whether the heroine, at the end of her first year as a teacher in a New York public school, should stay with her frantic and frustrating occupation, can be highlighted by asking students whether they themselves would accept the frustrations they have seen placed on some of their own teachers. A good assignment in this connection is to require students to compose letters in which they each impersonate one of their own teachers writing a letter of resignation, making sure they get into that letter a good picture of what students must seem to be like through that particular teacher's eyes. Such assignments would require students to focus on the potential for frustration in this line of work and at the same time could be used to get across certain rhetorical principles (such as the requirement for an essay to be appropriate to the character of the writer). On the other hand, students should also be required to picture moments of success in teaching. Finally, Kaufman's portrait of teaching can be readily compared to other descriptions of the same subject, either portraits found in other novels like Francis Gray Patton's *Good Morning, Miss Dove* and James Hilton's very different *Goodbye Mr. Chips*, or in treatments of teaching drawn from other genres. For besides novels, much modern drama, biography, and poetry have also dealt meaningfully with this subject.

Concerning poetry, however, I would like to point out that there are certain rather famous poems of special interest in the context of vocational decisions, specifically, poems that draw attention to the inevitable limitations one brings on oneself by choosing any particular occupation. These range from George Herbert's "The Collar," which portrays a preacher's struggle with religious discipline, to Wordsworth's sonnet, "Nuns Fret Not at Their Convent's Narrow Room," with its images of peace in confined tasks such as spinning, weaving, and even in studying. Imitations of such poems as these can prove challenging especially to talented pupils. On the other hand, class discussions in which students must bring up real-life instances of being limited and tied down by an occupation can also help in illuminating the poetry and in drawing attention to the great growth in personal character that is required in order for one to become skilled and successful in any significant or purposeful work. Indeed, it is almost impossible to overstress the importance of this particular theme. Some very fine literature exists which portrays the necessity for character in very different fields: Rölvaag's *Giants in the Earth*, for example, with its portrait of a long-suffering pioneer woman, or the dull but heroically conscientious ship captain of Conrad's *Typhoon*. Examples of this sort of literature could be multiplied, and a great many different aspects of personal character illustrated, from industry, perseverance, and patience to aggressiveness, courage, and self-sacrificing. However, a detailed discussion of an excellent short story by James Galsworthy can provide an illustration of such qualities as these, and it can also be used to raise the issue as to why character is needed at all, or whether it is primarily personal self-interest or some kind of principled cause for which one should be working in the first place.

This story, entitled "Quality"—and the quality of one's work is another issue which is very important for students to consider—is about a pair of German cobblers named Gessler working in England about the turn of the century. They make beautiful boots which are eminently well-fitted and long-lasting, attributes which result from the painstaking and particular attention the cobblers pay to the needs of each client's foot. Clearly their craft is an art to which they are extraordinarily devoted. However, as the story progresses, they are losing their customers to the sellers of factory-made boots. They have to reduce the size of their shop, which so saddens the elder Gessler that he dies as a result, and his younger brother progressively grows old before his time. But he continues making his boots, sitting over them day and night and putting all the money that he earns "back into rent and leather." Finally, the young, compassionate narrator, who has just received an order of boots and has found them to be the finest Gessler has ever made for him, goes into Gessler's shop to congratulate him, only to discover that it has been taken over by another man. This fellow tells him that Gessler has died, apparently from overwork and what the doctor calls "slow starvation," an outcome that he claims is all one could expect given Gessler's refusal to compromise, to advertise, or in any other way to submit to the demands of "progress."

Such, in short, is the plot of the story, and usually students feel one way or another about it, and especially about the younger of the two brothers. An excellent assignment is to have students write an argument proposing that the younger Gessler was a saint who gave his life for his work, or else was a fool who threw away his life needlessly, the story providing strong evidence for either proposition. Posing the issue in this way raises a great number of important questions. In general, and especially in our times, should one compromise quality and real concern for one's customers for the sake of one's own livelihood, losing one's self-respect in the process? Or, on the other hand, shouldn't one give the people what they actually want? What is the principal object of work—personal benefit or public service? And to what extent do modern conditions put a hiatus between these two objects? Finally one returns to the original question, whether the younger Gessler, who apparently consciously decided to do what he did, was courageous or cowardly, a saint and martyrlike figure or merely a stubborn old fool. Naturally, class discussion on these issues, perhaps involving the invention of modern parallels to Gessler's situation, or perhaps involving an ordered debate between the two sides, can prove to be stimulating and challenging to both teachers and students, especially if each person must learn to defend either view. And once again, the story is so composed that such an effort can only serve to shed light on the original text.

Other issues in literature can be approached in a similar fashion. But whatever the particular issue, or whatever the literary work, it is important to approach that work in a well-balanced way. In the foregoing example, for instance, we would be remiss if we did not point of the great worth of the cobbler's devotion to doing quality work; on the other hand, we could be equally faulted if we gave any less attention to the need for facing up to hard decisions and the necessity of dealing with the actualities with which as workers we will always be confronted, and which in the story Gessler seems to ignore. Similarly, in other cases. In considering

Mary Elizabeth Vroman's "See How They Run," for example, a short story about the success of a black schoolteacher against the odds of poverty, overloaded classes, and lack of student ambition, one could very properly ask how much of this teacher's success was due to her being young and enthusiastic, and how much of her vitality might fall off with age, when the frustrations might increase. With a depiction of failure such as is found in Ernest Hemingway's *The Old Man and the Sea*, one should point out that, as the text itself says, the old man "went out too far," and had he been perhaps a bit wiser, instead of leaving himself open to the tragedy that eventually occurs, he would have cut the line at the first. Of course, raising this latter alternative would challenge Hemingway's apparent intent, to glorify the old man's heroic struggle against enormous odds and certain defeat. But the philosophy Hemingway is preaching needs to be brought up in any full and sensitive teaching of the book, and certainly no philosophy, Hemingway's no less than any other, should be held immune from criticism.

Our attitude, then, in dealing with all literature involving work, needs to be one of allowing that meaningful and constructive results are usually possible and are greatly to be desired and sought for. But recognition must be given to the fact that the attainment of these results will require intense, painful, and sometimes desperate effort. It is true that a great number of modern works of literature exist which, instead of portraying the possibilities for meaning in work, suggest that there is no hope and that all laborious effort is futile. Certainly we must be alive to the possibilities for frustration and alienation and must give works manifesting such difficulties and hopelessness full consideration, for there is no question that they reflect certain realities about our culture and our experience. But failure and frustration in portraits of work is often the fruit of failure of vision and perserverance—in the character or in the author. Usually, if looked at carefully, every work situation will embody some kind of meaning and potential, a potential which we must support. Put in other terms, while it is true that literature portraying the frustrations to be found in modern work, like the frustrations to be found in modern life as a whole, will always be with us in superabundance, *for this very reason* it is incumbent upon us to offer our students, along with such material, whatever we can also offer in the way of vision, purpose, and meaning. Specifically, we must offer them images of purposeful work being done, of hope, and of substantial achievement. Willy Loman they will see all their lives; Madame Curie they will not meet every day. And if they do not meet Madame Curie in our classes, or Willa Cather's archbishop and singer, or William Gibson's *The Miracle Worker* or even James Herriot's humorous vet, they are unlikely to meet them at all. More important, we won't be meeting them either. And it may well be that the greatest value of a serious attempt at teaching English with an eye to the possibility of meaningful work and vocation would be the revitalization of our own work and a rededication to our own vocation.

Note

1. John Dos Passos, *U.S.A.* (New York: Random House, 1937), pp. 430–33.

Stimulating Writing
Through Job Awareness

Alan McLeod
Virginia Commonwealth University

From their excursion into the business community, the author
and a group of English teachers discovered that many of the
general skills and attributes employers consider important parallel
the skills and attitudes we try to teach in the language arts classroom. As a result of this investigation, participants derived a
lengthy list of ideas for writing as it is related to jobs and the
community.

What does the business community expect of prospective employees? What resources in the business community might be used
for instructional purposes? What might be done in a secondary
school classroom to enhance student success in seeking and retain-
ing jobs? These were three of the questions twenty-one teachers
and guidance counselors and one university professor posed during
a recent inservice program. Our investigation led us to local and
national industries and businesses, a science museum, a spider
museum, the Folger Library, and many other locations. In the
process we discovered a number of possibilities for writing experiences, field trips, and career education.

Participants were continually amazed at how well they were
received by the business community—a community which was
impressed that teachers would make the effort to explore how
businesses function and what attributes are important in seeking
employment. We found many of the expectations of business were
pertinent to English classes. Those responsible for hiring stated
skills and attributes they desired in an applicant, including the
ability to spell conventionally, punctuate appropriately, and write

This article was originally published in the *English Journal*, vol. 67
(November 1978), pp. 42-43. Copyright © 1978 by the National Council of
Teachers of English. Reprinted by permission of the author and publisher.

sentences in which subjects and verbs agree; ability to write legibly, follow directions, pay attention to details; ability to communicate clearly orally; and accuracy. Also given considerable importance were attendance, including limited tardiness; ability to work well with others; attitudes and manners; pride in work; appropriate attire; demonstration of respect; willingness to accept responsibility; promptness/punctuality; realistic expectations about the type of job for which one qualifies and its pay scale; computation ability; knowledge of previous work experience, including dates of employment and employers; a sense of how to participate in an interview; and reliability.

The more of these skills and attributes one possesses, the greater the opportunity for being employed. While the subject of "grammar" was mentioned in several interviews, no one used it in the sense of nomenclature or the identification of nouns and participles. What was stressed was subject-verb agreement, usage, and the ability to express oneself clearly. These are matters which may be addressed in various classrooms, as are hints to successful job seeking: attire, manners, interviewing, punctuality, realistic expectations, and so forth.

At the end of the experience, one teacher concluded: "We found out that first impressions are important and social graces still count a good deal in a job interview." Another stated, "It was really amazing the number of employers who pointed out that the attitude of the prospective employee is as important as the skills for the job." Still another participant was surprised that *identification* of such items as subjects and verbs in sentences was not of consequence (but that agreement of subject and verb was highly important). Most educators were impressed, too, with the broad range of jobs, the skills they require, and the recognition that teachers can help students develop these skills in their own classes. They were impressed as well with the reception they were given and the resources available in the community to support the learning situations developed in the classroom. At the end of the experience, the educators were identifying business, industry, and community resources their students could visit as well as those which could be brought into the classroom. As one teacher noted, "It may be that incorporating career education in my classes is not so difficult; at least I have a positive idea of where I can *begin*."

One of the more important gleanings of this experience was the recognition of additional purpose to be given in stimulating student writing. The business letter achieved new dimensions in some minds, as did the following oral and written activities:

1. structuring interviews in the classroom;
2. exploring the social and economic pay off of using standard English;
3. writing letters inquiring about job possibilities;
4. responding to want ads in writing;
5. preparing resumes;
6. completing application forms;
7. reading about job requirements and expectations;
8. drafting job descriptions;
9. writing reports on skills needed in different types of jobs;
10. interviewing managers of businesses, from fast food restaurants to broom makers to poultry processors to funeral directors to personnel officers in corporations;
11. reporting in oral and written forms on jobs students have held or hope to hold;
12. exploring the impact of one's oral and written language and computation skills on prospective employers;
13. writing stories about jobs which may not now exist;
14. keeping journals about jobs, the people met, the pleasures and frustrations;
15. writing autobiographies emphasizing employment;
16. developing editorials about students and jobs for the school paper;
17. composing letters to the editor of a local paper concerning jobs or employee characteristics;
18. writing plays or radio or television scripts set in job situations;
19. writing newspaper stories about people and jobs;
20. writing advertisements and commercials;
21. developing plans and materials for career awareness days;
22. drafting telegrams;
23. writing reviews of books about jobs;
24. drawing cartoons about jobs;
25. researching the economy or the job market or the need for different types of jobs;
26. writing about successful and unsuccessful interviews;

27. editing copy for publishing;
28. setting up a mock business;
29. writing letters of introduction;
30. writing letters of recommendation;
31. writing responses to advertisements;
32. interviewing workers in various types of jobs, including family members and neighbors;
33. preparing lists of items to purchase at the grocery store or supplies for a business and setting up an imaginary checking account;
34. assisting with inventories of school supplies.

The list could, of course, proceed with many other possibilities for writing, reading, listening and speaking. Many adolescents look for jobs; others anticipate jobs in the future; others need to become more aware of job opportunities. A focus exists for stimulating student writing and other skills activities—and a context is set for helping students understand the necessity of being able to use, as appropriate, standard English, including conventions of spelling and punctuation. Writing about the job market, including desirable skills and procedures, appears to be an important—and legitimate—means, among others, of stimulating student writing.

The Daily Newspaper: A Text for the Language Arts and Career Education

Reta Broadway
Newspaper in Education Program,
The Courier-Journal and *The Louisville Times*

Utilizing the daily newspaper, students in the language arts class-room at any level can develop self-awareness, career awareness, and appreciation for work itself and the variety of career options available to them. By focusing on career education goals through the newspaper while learning and practicing language arts skills, students can discover new and important meanings for language arts, the newspaper, and career education.

If career education seeks to give students an opportunity to prepare for success in the real world, then what better material for teaching can there be than the journal of the real world—the daily newspaper? For language arts teachers the newspaper offers an ideal opportunity for integrating skills development in reading, writing, and oral expression with career education.

One way of dividing career education into its various components is to use the following terms: career awareness, self-awareness, appreciations and attitudes, decision making, economic awareness, skills awareness, employability skills, and education awareness. The newspaper can be used as a teaching material in each of these areas, but its applicability is more obvious in some than in others. Three of the areas—career awareness, self-awareness, and appreciations and attitudes—constitute the focus of this article, since the possibilities for using the newspaper in each of them may be less readily recognized by language arts teachers.

The activities suggested here can be adapted by language arts teachers at all grade levels. Repeating an activity will provide students with new information and insight because of the constantly changing content of the newspaper.

Career Awareness

As language arts teachers work with students in developing literal comprehension skills in reading newspaper articles, they can consciously select news items and feature stories that explore various occupations, especially those that are available in the students' immediate community. Once discussion about job availability has surfaced in the classroom, an immediate follow-up is a scanning lesson in the classified ads. Students will gain practice in an important reading skill while gathering information that will give their career exploration a sense of immediate practicality.

The newspaper can also be used to look at the job market from a different perspective. By collecting news items and feature articles of both local and national origin, students can search out the unusual occupations that play a part in society. These same articles can serve as a basis for developing skills in comparison and contrast as students compare the kinds of jobs and professions existing in their community with those that exist in other communities.

Newspaper articles that are clipped for these activities can become the basis of a career file, an ongoing collection of information about work possibilities. Having such a career file in the language arts classroom not only provides interesting, pertinent reading material for students, but it also serves as a convenient resource for researching questions that will come up during a study of careers.

The newspaper is a reflection of the state of career sex-role stereotyping that persists in society today. In addition to reading news items, investigative articles, and editorials that directly address this question, there are indirect ways of examining it as well. One activity involves having students scan specific pages of the newspaper for roles that are assigned to people and to note these roles. They can note whether the roles are specifically associated with a man or a woman. Having accumulated a variety of roles, they are ready to isolate those that are related to life work and analyze this reduced list in terms of sex-role assignment. An activity such as this gives students experience in critical thinking and analysis as well as sensitizing them to the difficulties that may still exist for workers who choose careers considered nontraditional for their sex. Another value in such a newspaper research project is that it makes students aware of any preconceived sex roles they themselves may attribute to specific careers. For language arts teachers a discussion based on the results of these activities is an excellent opportunity for a vivid lesson in differentiating between fact and opinion.

Self-Awareness

This point brings us squarely into the second of the three aspects of career education—self-awareness. To make even tentative career choices students must be able to articulate their own deepest values, interests, and abilities and be able to relate these to life work options. The language arts teacher, as humanist, is in an ideal situation to promote this self-awareness in students, and once again the newspaper provides a number of timely experiences for such growth.

For younger students, making "look at me" collages—words, photos, and other items from the newspaper that reflect the individual personalities of students—can be the beginning of both self-awareness and self-assertion. The same type of activity can be carried on at a more sophisticated level with older students by having them list their most important values and then find news articles and other features that support or come into conflict with those values. In addition to providing values clarification experiences, language arts teachers can use these activities as opportunities for reinforcing classification skills and enhancing discussion techniques.

Another values clarification activity is to have students select pictures or names of items from the newspaper that they consider necessary to their lives and other items that they very much want. They can write a short explanation of how their personal lists of needs and wants might affect their career decisions.

Having students identify articles, photos, and ads that arouse certain emotions also helps to focus self-awareness. This identification can be done using a sentence-completion technique, where students find information in the newspaper to complete sentences such as the following:

> I am surprised that . . .
>
> I am relieved that . . .
>
> I am amused that . . .
>
> I am angry that . . .

Examining cartoon strips can also be an exercise in self-awareness. While using the comics to teach inferential comprehension skills, context clue usage, and aspects of humor, language arts teachers can also encourage students to pay special attention to what seems funny or poignant or repugnant to them. By watching their own responses to comics, students can become more conscious of stereotypes, patterns of human nature, and significant cultural habits.

By encouraging students to follow a controversial issue through an extended period of newspaper coverage, language arts teachers can nurture the critical ability to examine facts in relation to one's own values and to make decisions that are both intelligent and ethical. Students can clip all the information they can find on a subject and analyze the material for points on both sides of a controversy. It is the teacher's responsibility to make sure that all forms of information are included whether these are news stories, editorials, cartoons, or advertisements. After analyzing the information in light of their own values, the students are in a position to make decisions about the issue. Here again, language arts teachers play a significant role in helping the students articulate that stand.

When students have been together awhile, they can see how well they have communicated themselves to their classmates by making "look at me" collages and leaving their names off. Then the class can try to identify which collages belong to which individuals. Follow-up discussions can examine those aspects of the individual's personality that are readily apparent, those that are less obvious, and to what degree students have communicated these aspects of themselves.

Reacting to advice given by syndicated advice columnists also gives students a change to form and express their own opinions on contemporary problems. Similarly, syndicated opinion columns from the op-ed page and letters to the editor provide topics of interest and importance to students in collecting, formulating, supporting, and defending their values and beliefs.

There are other newspaper-oriented experiences that create thought-provoking situations for students.

> Have students select a person in the news whom they consider to have heroic qualities. Involve the students in class discussions about the qualities they consider heroic, the contemporary people who possess those qualities, and the opportunities in modern life for demonstrating heroism. Encourage students to look for examples of heroism associated with professional life. Try to discover if they perceive certain careers as being particularly heroic.

Have students write newspaper ads to sell themselves. Vary this idea by having them create both classified ads and display ads or by having them put together different ads to appear in different sections of the paper, each reflecting the general content of those sections.

Assign students the writing of obituaries—their own. To encourage an outlook toward the future, have them write one obituary that might appear if they died today and another that they would like to have appear if they die when they are ninety years old. Discuss with the students the part played by careers in the second obituary. Have them consider to what extent they see the next decades of their lives shaped by their careers, whether they imagine themselves having several careers during their lives, and if there are other ways in which the imaginary obituaries reflect possible careers.

Make a "winners and losers" bulletin board in your classroom that students can complete with items clipped from newspapers. They can include examples from news stories, features, ads, comic strips, and business and sports sections. Use the bulletin board to initiate discussions on students' conceptions of "winners and losers"—the causes, the benefits, and the side effects of winning or losing.

Have students create comic strips about themselves. Or let them select existing comic-strip characters with whom they can identify and explain the reasons for their selections.

Appreciations and Attitudes

As students become knowledgeable about the work that is available and more attuned to their own values and interests, they begin to develop appreciations and attitudes about different kinds of work. Here again, language arts teachers will find the newspaper a pertinent, timely source for enhancing this development. Starting with the perceptions of the work world that students already hold, language arts teachers can lead brainstorming sessions on the reasons why people work. Beyond sheer financial survival, what do people expect from their jobs? When students have compiled a list of reasons for working, they can reexamine the newspaper articles they have collected in the career file for indications of what jobs best meet various needs.

Another interesting way of looking at the need-fulfillment

aspects of careers is to analyze the comic strips. First, have students divide the comics into those in which the main characters have careers and those in which a career is not evident. Discuss the degree to which the career-oriented characters are integrally involved in their jobs. What satisfactions and frustrations do they seem to derive from their careers? What aspects of the job world are exaggerated or unrealistically portrayed in comic strips, and why are these projections put forth as humorous? What does the presence of career identification in comic strips say about the part careers play in people's lives? What attitudes are generally expressed toward jobs?

After the comic pages, students can progress to the real world of the news and feature pages of the newspaper and perform the same kind of analysis. Many feature articles are written to describe people in unusual professions or people who have added new dimensions to familiar jobs. Often these articles speak specifically to the benefits a person perceives in a career; in other instances, these benefits are implied. For language arts teachers, such stories provide an opportunity for sharpening literal and inferential comprehension skills while sensitizing students to the satisfactions that can be derived from different careers.

Feature articles frequently detail a person's involvement with hobbies, and examining these gives rise to two additional considerations for students. First, students can be encouraged to think about the range of their own interests, whether they have hobbies to which they will want to devote large blocks of time, whether their careers will have to provide them with money to support costly hobbies, whether a hobby itself can become a money-making project. The other consideration is whether a hobby is rewarding and important enough to make into a career, a focal point of the individual's work world.

An alternative way of doing this type of analysis is to read news and feature articles about what is important to people outside of their careers, to identify the values and interests in these non-career activities, and then to match up the newsmakers with careers that might fulfill some of the same criteria. A variation of this activity is to have students select fifteen jobs listed in the classified ads and list as many benefits as they can for each job. Going one step further, students can select the one job in fifteen that offers the benefits most significant to them.

The ways in which careers are perceived by those other than the individuals who hold them are evident in many newspaper items. Editorials, letters to the editor, columns, and feature stories all from time to time carry observations and opinions about different careers. Identifying these attitudes, comparing them with one's own, and checking out the accuracy of them will help to develop students' critical and evaluative thinking skills as well as make them aware of their own feelings about the attitudes of others.

Here is the place where students can examine the degree to which their personal career choices are impinged upon by others' opinions. Does being a doctor or lawyer appeal to one student only because everyone else in the family is in one of these professions? Is another student ready to give up the dream of owning a greenhouse because friends see that as a strange ambition? Language arts teachers can help students to be conscious of society's influence so that they can make career decisions based on the greatest possible self-awareness.

Another aspect of appreciations and attitudes lies in helping students see the value in careers other than those that are of personal interest to them. The newspaper can be the source of an interesting activity along these lines. Over a period of days students can collect newspaper stories in which a particular kind of work is central to the importance of the story. Students can then pick a few of these stories and write their own news items about the imagined elimination of the career and the implications that this elimination would have for their society. What, in fact, would happen to the world as we know it if scuba divers, street cleaners, or sign painters suddenly were no longer workers in our society?

Students can also use their increased familiarity with journalistic style to interview people in their lives about work and write feature and news articles about the personal aspects of different kinds of work. Besides giving students practice in interview techniques and factual writing, this activity provides them with firsthand information about the satisfactions, frustrations, and importance of different careers. These news articles can be collected in a class newspaper on careers and kept as a resource along with the career file.

Becoming familiar with the newspaper is a valuable language arts objective in itself. All the suggestions made in this article use the newspaper to teach reading, writing, and oral language skills while deliberately emphasizing career awareness, self-awareness, and attitudes toward and appreciations of various careers. Language arts teachers can create many other activities based on the newspaper that will provide their students at every grade level with both practical and humanistic skills in all areas of career education.

The Young Adult Novel and Career Education: Another Kind of Relevance

Marjorie M. Kaiser
University of Louisville

The author proposes that contemporary young adult novels, like standard literature, can serve as a basis for student inquiry into the role of work in human lives. Because of their easy readability, their emphasis on timely themes, and their potential for identification and response, they can also reinforce a variety of basic career education concepts.

In the last few years a great many language arts teachers at the middle and high school levels have responded to the call of career education advocates by agreeing to teach work-related communication skills, such as those required in interviewing, writing resumes, completing application forms, and so forth. At the high school level, English teachers have long been willing to offer and teach courses in business English or vocational English and to participate annually in such occasions as Career Day. But few have been sanguine about diluting, or polluting, the literature-study portion of the English program with career education. For some reason, even though English teachers invariably list "student self-understanding" and "understanding of the human condition" as goals of the teaching of literature, it seems a sacrilege to many to integrate career education and literature study.

Yet, these two disciplines are a natural combination, for a great deal of literature treats the subject of work and treats it with a depth and breadth not available through other means. The kind of work a literary character does is not always a crucial factor in the artist's representation of life, but it often is. Throughout the history of literature, work as a concept has been featured prominently as a concern of the literary artist, and the work of individual characters has regularly been shown to shape a character as well as to be shaped by that character's human values, personal traits, and needs. From Chaucer's pilgrims to Hawthorne's scientists and and clergymen, from Shakespeare's rulers, merchants, and warriors to Melville's seamen, scriveners, and lawyers, from Wordsworth's Michael to Steinbeck's migrant workers and laborers of all types, from Dreiser and Crane to Arthur Miller and Tennessee Williams, from Walt Whitman to Harper Lee, the work characters in literature do is important, in varying degrees, to the kinds of people they are. Likewise, characters have unique impacts on the kinds of work they do.

This interaction can be explored by knowing working individuals intimately, but how many individuals can one know well enough to gain the depth and breadth of understanding desirable in learning how work of any kind affects the humanness of the person and how his or her humanness affects the work? Probably very few. Through reading and discussing literature, a student can gain a deeper understanding of this important but neglected aspect of career education. This kind of knowledge is not factual in the way that much career education knowledge is, such as salary projections or specific job skill requirements. It is, however, significant to *all* students, who *must* consider themselves as human beings, whether their career expectations include being a doctor, an assembly-line worker, or an insurance salesman.

Popular young adult fiction has the same potential as more standard literature, such as I have already mentioned. Because of their readability, their immediate appeal, and their potential for easy identification for middle and high school students, young adult novels could serve us even better than standard literature for the integration of career education and literature study. In addition to the many other good reasons for enjoying these novels, through them students can explore the meaning of work, the interaction between individuals and their work, and the effects of a person's work on those around him or her.

For the purpose of this article, I do not refer to the so-called career books or biographies and autobiographies of individuals famous in their fields of endeavor, though these books may be both good literature and inspirational accounts and could be extremely helpful in providing students with information, opportunities for vicarious experiences, and models. Rather, I will focus on the potential of young adult novels.

To begin with, while work or careers is rarely a dominant theme in contemporary young adult novels, many of the books in this genre present a variety of characters involved in the world of work. While principal characters are most often adolescents, not themselves employed, they are frequently surrounded by parents, friends, other adults, and acquaintances who are part of the work force. We find teachers, doctors, business managers, nurses, farmers, police officers, pharmacists, social workers, writers, and others. And often, the work these individuals do and the attitudes they have toward their work have a direct bearing on the attitudes and behavior of the principal character.

We find, for example, a number of psychiatrists, such as Dr. Berger in Judith Guest's *Ordinary People* (1976), Dr. Donovan in *Lisa, Bright and Dark* (1970) by John Neufeld, and Dr. Fried in Hannah Green's *I Never Promised You a Rose Garden* (1973). We meet businessmen such as Mr. Pete Degley in Mildred Lee's *The Skating Rink* (1970), George Diener in Thomas Thompson's *Richie* (1974), and Leo, David's father in Barbara Wersba's *Run Softly, Go Fast* (1972). Teachers of many varieties appear in these popular adolescent novels—Nigeria Green in Alice Childress's *A Hero Ain't Nothin' But a Sandwich* (1974), Justin in Isabelle Holland's *The Man Without a Face* (1973), and the array of teacher-priests in Robert Cormier's *The Chocolate War* (1975).

It is true that in many cases the glimpses the reader gets of some workers may be so brief that these characters appear flat and/or stereotyped. Anyone can imagine how police officers are often portrayed in novels told from an adolescent rebel's point of view. A good example of this particular stereotype is the impression of the police a reader may get from one of Paul Zindel's latest efforts, *Confessions of a Teenage Baboon* (1977).

It is also true that in some novels parents or other adults are portrayed as so involved in their careers that they cease to function effectively in their other human roles, especially in the parent role in relation to the struggling adolescent principal character. This is certainly the case in Glendon Swarthout's *Bless the Beasts and Children* (1973), in Barbara Wersba's *Run Softly, Go Fast* (1972), in Kin Platt's *The Boy Who Could Make Himself Disappear* (1971), in M. E. Kerr's *The Son of Someone Famous* (1975) and *Dinky Hocker Shoots Smack* (1972), and in many others.

Some young adult novels feature young adults already functioning full time in the world of work. Through such works as Margaret Craven's *I Heard the Owl Call My Name* (1973), Ronald Glasser's *Ward 402* (1973), or the James Herriot novels (*All Creatures Great and Small* [1972], and the others), readers get an in-depth view of the interaction between individuals and their work. They can learn the meaning of dedication to one's work as well as appreciate the hardships and difficult decisions associated with certain kinds of work.

In some young adult novels both plot and theme center on the principal character's struggle toward a career decision. Sometimes the character is helped by adults, but sometimes he or she is hindered. Several books that illustrate this theme are Beverly Butler's *Gift of Gold* (1973), Barbara Wersba's *Run Softly, Go Fast* (1972), and Ursula LeGuin's *Very Far Away from Anywhere Else* (1976). In this LeGuin novel, career decision making really is the heart of the story. Owen Griffiths and Natalie Field, very bright seniors in high school, develop a loving friendship based on their common goal to "do something challenging and creative with their future lives," he in science, she as a composer of music.

And there are novels in which parents and other adults function effectively and happily in their work and manage to maintain positive and supportive relationships with the young people with whom they regularly interact. Think of Norma Klein's *Mom, The Wolfman, and Me* (1974), Robert Peck's *A Day No Pigs Would Die* (1974), and Virginia Hamilton's *M. C. Higgins, the Great* (1974).

And finally, there are novels that directly question the need to achieve fulfillment through one's work—indeed, that even challenge the value of work itself. Alice Childress's *A Hero Ain't Nothin' But a Sandwich* (1974) and Frankcina Glass's *Marvin and Tige* (1977) are just two excellent illustrations of this viewpoint.

Whether the impressions readers get of the world of work and individuals participating in it are positive or negative is really not very important. What is important is that the idea of work is there in a great many young adult novels, often impinges directly on both character and theme, and asks to be noticed and discussed. The idea of work itself speaks to adolescent readers as they contemplate their futures. Adolescents are *much* concerned with how they will earn a living and are ready to know what kinds of work they would like to be qualified for, what work will bring them the kinds of rewards they seek, and how work may affect them as human beings.

In addition to providing fertile ground for exploring work and its meaning to the individual and society, contemporary young adult novels can be a means of reinforcing certain career education concepts. Although the junior high or middle school is typically designated as the exploratory phase in most career education programs, there should be nothing to prevent exploration from continuing during the high school years. Career education concepts appropriate to the exploratory phase and appropriate to what might be communicated through literature rather than through actual work experience are presented below. Several titles of popular young adult novels are listed beneath each concept.

Contemporary Young Adult Novels and Selected Career Education Concepts Appropriate to the Exploratory Phase

Concept 1—There is dignity in work.

Craven, Margaret. *I Heard the Owl Call My Name*
Hamilton, Virginia. *M. C. Higgins, the Great*
————. *Zeely*
Herriot, James. *All Creatures Great and Small*
Klein, Norma. *Mom, the Wolfman, and Me*
Lee, Mildred. *The Skating Rink*
Lipsyte, Robert. *The Contender*
Peck, Robert. *A Day No Pigs Would Die*
Zindel, Paul. *Confessions of a Teenage Baboon*

Concept 2—Persons need to be recognized as having dignity and worth.

Fox, Paula. *The Slave Dancer*
Jordan, June. *His Own Where*
Kerr, M. E. *Dinky Hocker Shoots Smack*
————. *The Son of Someone Famous*
Neufeld, John. *Lisa, Bright and Dark*
Platt, Kin. *The Boy Who Could Make Himself Disappear*
————. *Hey, Dummy*
Sleator, William. *House of Stairs*
Swarthout, Glendon. *Bless the Beasts and Children*

Concept 3—Society is dependent upon the work of many people.

Butterworth, W. E. *Susan and Her Classic Convertible*
Cleaver, Vera, and Cleaver, Bill. *Where the Lilies Bloom*
Eyerly, Jeanette. *Bonnie Jo, Go Home*
Glass, Frankcina. *Marvin and Tige*
Jordan, June. *His Own Where*

Concept 4—Work means different things to different people.

Glass, Frankcina. *Marvin and Tige*
Kerr, M. E. *The Son of Someone Famous*
Lee, Mildred. *The Skating Rink*

Lipsyte, Robert. *The Contender*
Wojciechowska, Maia. *A Single Light*
Zindel, Paul. *I Never Loved Your Mind*

Concept 5—An understanding and acceptance of self is important throughout life.

Blume, Judy. *Deenie*
Donovan, John. *I'll Get There, It Better Be Worth the Trip*
Glass, Frankcina. *Marvin and Tige*
Guest, Judith. *Ordinary People*
Holland, Isabelle. *Love and Death and Other Journeys*
————. *The Man without a Face*
Hinton, S. E. *That Was Then, This is Now*
LeGuin, Ursula. *Very Far Away from Anywhere Else*
Lipsyte, Robert. *The Contender*
Neufeld, John. *For All the Wrong Reasons*

Concept 6—Individuals differ in their interests, abilities, attitudes, and values.

Childress, Alice. *A Hero Ain't Nothin' But a Sandwich*
Cormier, Robert. *The Chocolate War*
Craven, Margaret. *I Heard the Owl Call My Name*
Glass, Frankcina. *Marvin and Tige*
LeGuin, Ursula. *Very Far Away from Anywhere Else*
Zindel, Paul. *The Pigman*

Concept 7—Education and work are interrelated.

Butler, Beverly. *Gift of Gold*
Childress, Alice. *A Hero Ain't Nothin' But a Sandwich*
Glasser, Ronald J. *Ward 402*
Herriot, James. *All Creatures Great and Small*
Holland, Isabelle. *The Man without a Face*
LeGuin, Ursula. *Very Far Away from Anywhere Else*
Neufeld, John. *For All the Wrong Reasons*

Concept 8—The occupation one chooses affects one's total lifestyle.

Craven, Margaret. *I Heard the Owl Call My Name*
Hall, Lynn. *Sticks and Stones*
LeGuin, Ursula. *Very Far Away from Anywhere Else*
Thompson, Thomas. *Richie*
Wersba, Barbara. *Run Softly, Go Fast*
Wojciechowska, Maia. *A Single Light*
Zindel, Paul. *Confessions of a Teenage Baboon*

Concept 9—Satisfying and rewarding work may bring fulfillment.

Cleaver, Vera, and Cleaver, Bill. *Where the Lilies Bloom*
Craven, Margaret. *I Heard the Owl Call My Name*
Herriot, James. *All Creatures Great and Small*
Lipsyte, Robert. *The Contender*
Peck, Robert. *A Day No Pigs Would Die*
Rawls, Wilson. *Where the Red Fern Grows*

Concept 10—Such factors as age, sex, race, or religion no longer limit career possibilities.

Blume, Judy. *Forever*
Butterworth, W. E. *Susan and Her Classic Convertible*
Glass, Frankcina. *Marvin and Tige*
Hamilton, Virginia. *M. C. Higgins, the Great*
Holland, Isabelle. *Love and Death and Other Journeys*
LeGuin, Ursula. *Very Far Away from Anywhere Else*
O'Brien, Robert C. *Z for Zachariah*

As can be seen by a quick glance at this list, some of the concepts—numbers 2, 5, and 6 in particular—are so broad as to be unrelated to work per se. Still, they are excellent concepts that English teachers would agree need to be reinforced and can be reinforced very easily, if indirectly, through a great many young adult novels. I do not propose that English teachers present a young adult novel primarily as a vehicle for the inculcating of concepts or the preaching of certain value systems, though many do just that unabashedly on their own.

In the October 1978 *Kappan*, Maia Mertz, in an article entitled "The New Realism: Traditional Cultural Values in Recent Young Adult Fiction," contends that popular young adult novels typically reinforce conventional values and attitudes. Mertz states: "The majority of current young adult books that have been labeled as controversial are not controversial at all if the reader looks beneath the unconventional plots and sometimes atypical characters. Even though the books might employ characters, settings, and lifestyles that were not included in earlier novels for young adults, the dominant themes not only uphold but also reinforce traditional values and beliefs." Among these traditional beliefs are the convictions that work has dignity and that hard work can be both rewarding and ennobling.

It would seem foolish to avoid the importance of work in relation to theme and characterization when it is there. Work is an important part of almost everyone's life, and adolescents want to and need to explore the idea through their own lives and through fiction. Where stereotypes exist, these need to be examined; where devotion to careers stifle individual and family happiness, questions need to be raised; where work is fulfilling, notice must be taken; where the value of work itself is suspect, exchange of ideas and clarification are in order.

Through directed reading, classroom discussion, and other activities, students can explore and question, think and dream, compare their own feelings and uncertainties about their present and future work in the world with their fictional counterparts. Through young adult novels, they can develop self-insight and understanding that is not now available through current formal career education programs and probably never can be.

References

Articles

Kaiser, Marjorie. "Unintended Career Education in the English Classroom." *Journal of Career Education* 3 (Spring 1977): 14-24.

Mertz, Maia. "The New Realism: Traditional Cultural Values in Recent Young Adult Fiction." *Phi Delta Kappan* 60 (October 1978): 101-5.

Books

Blume, Judy. *Deenie.* New York: Dell, 1974.

—————. *Forever.* New York: Pocket Books, 1974.

Butler, Beverly. *Gift of Gold.* New York: Pocket Books, 1973.

Butterworth, W. E. *Susan and Her Classic Convertible.* New York: Four Winds, 1970.

Childress, Alice. *A Hero Ain't Nothin' But a Sandwich.* New York: Avon, 1974.

Cleaver, Vera, and Cleaver, Bill. *Where the Lilies Bloom.* New York: New American Library, 1974.

Cormier, Robert. *The Chocolate War.* New York: Dell, 1975.

Craven, Margaret. *I Heard the Owl Call My Name.* New York: Doubleday, 1973.

Donovan, John. *I'll Get There, It Better Be Worth the Trip.* New York: Dell, 1969.

Eyerly, Jeanette. *Bonnie Jo, Go Home.* New York: Bantam, 1973.

Fox, Paula. *The Slave Dancer.* New York: Dell, 1975.

Glass, Frankcina. *Marvin and Tige.* New York: St. Martin's Press, 1977.

Glasser, Ronald. *Ward 402.* New York: Pocket Books, 1973.

Green, Hannah. *I Never Promised You a Rose Garden.* New York: New American Library, 1973.

Guest, Judith. *Ordinary People.* New York: Ballantine, 1976.

Hall, Lynn. *Sticks and Stones.* New York: Dell, 1972.

Hamilton, Virginia. *M. C. Higgins, the Great.* New York: Macmillan, 1974.

————. *Zeely.* New York: Dell, 1978.

Herriot, James. *All Creatures Great and Small.* New York: St Martin's Press, 1972.

Hinton, S. E. *That Was Then, This Is Now.* New York: Dell, 1972.

Holland, Isabelle. *Love and Death and Other Journeys.* Philadelphia: Lippincott, 1975.

————. *The Man without a Face.* New York: Bantam, 1973.

Jordan, June. *His Own Where.* New York: Dell, 1973.

Kerr, M. E. *Dinky Hocker Shoots Smack.* New York: Harper & Row, 1972.

————. *The Son of Someone Famous.* New York: Ballantine, 1975.

Klein, Norma. *Mom, the Wolfman, and Me.* New York: Avon, 1974.

Lee, Mildred. *The Skating Rink.* New York: Dell, 1970.

LeGuin, Ursula. *Very Far Away from Anywhere Else.* New York: Atheneum, 1976.

Lipsyte, Robert. *The Contender.* New York: Bantam, 1969.

Neufeld, John. *Lisa, Bright and Dark.* New York: New American Library, 1970.

————. *For All the Wrong Reasons.* New York: New American Library, 1974.

O'Brien, Robert C. *Z for Zachariah.* New York: Atheneum, 1975.

Peck, Robert. *A Day No Pigs Would Die.* New York: Dell, 1974.

Platt, Kin. *The Boy Who Could Make Himself Disappear.* New York: Dell, 1971.

————. *Hey, Dummy.* New York: Dell, 1973.

Rawls, Wilson. *Where the Red Fern Grows.* New York: Bantam, 1974.

Sleator, William. *House of Stairs.* New York: Dutton, 1974.

Swarthout, Glendon. *Bless the Beasts and Children.* New York: Pocket Books, 1973.

Thompson, Thomas. *Richie.* New York: Bantam: 1974.

Wersba, Barbara. *Run Softly, Go Fast.* New York: Bantam, 1972.

Wojciechowska, Maia. *A Single Light.* New York: Bantam, 1971.

Zindel, Paul. *Confessions of a Teenage Baboon.* New York: Bantam, 1977.

————. *I Never Loved Your Mind.* New York: Bantam, 1972.

————. *The Pigman.* New York: Harper & Row, 1968.

IV English, Career Education, and the Future

Two Worlds But One Universe: Teachers of English and Corporate Communications

Glenn Leggett
Deere and Company, Moline, Illinois, retired

As a person with extensive professional experience in both the academic and corporate worlds, the author presents a unique perspective on English teachers' responsibility to be concerned with the relevance of their instruction to students' future work lives. The need for collaborative efforts between the academic and business worlds is also convincingly underscored.

I want to say something here about the world of corporate communications and about the world of teachers of English—and thus, indirectly at least, something about the need for a more sensible relationship between the two worlds, so that the teaching of English as a part of career education can be more effective.

In one of Agatha Christie's mysteries, a leading British banker is explaining how he progressed from being a lowly bank clerk to his present position:

> "Well, if I read something that is written down in English, *I can understand what it means*—I am not talking of abstruse stuff, formulae, or philosophy—just plain businesslike English—*most people can't!* If I want to write something down, *I can write down what I mean*—I've discovered that quite a lot of people can't do that, either!"[1]

The statement suggests at least two things about communication skills. First, the corporate world tends to move on words. Second, the words it moves on are not those written and spoken by teachers of English language arts; they are the words of those who

---

[1] To keep things in perspective, we need the rest of the banker's explanation: "And, as I say, I can do plain arithmetic. If Jones has eight bananas and Brown takes ten away from him, how many will Jones have left? That's the kind of sum people like to pretend has a simple answer. They won't admit, first, that Brown can't do it—and, second, that there won't be an answer in plus bananas!"

read and write business letters and reports, and those who give and listen to explanations and directives. That is, they are the words of personnel directors, works managers, marketing researchers, accountants, purchasing agents, comptrollers, salary administrators, production controllers, labor negotiators, plant and product engineers, and marketing and manufacturing persons of dozens of different descriptions. If there are any college speech or writing majors in this assortment, they hide their identities behind more immediately acceptable kinds of training and experience.

These facts of the matter bother English teachers, especially composition teachers. It appears to diminish their importance in the scheme of things; their pride suffers. More importantly, they dislike being misunderstood. For, in truth, the real-world activities that make reading and writing such crucial skills have always been understood by most teachers. They would like the world to know that they know. Their use of the "theme" and the "oral report" are only convenient pedagogical devices, and their assignments in literary analysis and current events are mostly reflections of their own taste and training. Teachers are sure that their bright and purposeful students, whatever their present interests, will eventually awaken fully to the real-world importance of what has been taught. Their frustration comes partly from their inability to cut through teenage confusions and so speed up the waking process— and partly, of course, from their continuing public image as amiable but rather unworldly types.

For their part, corporate communicators are also uneasy. They know that in the corporation very few hard questions about reading and writing are asked of threshold applicants, except of secretaries, advertising copywriters, and press or publication specialists. Other applicants are mostly judged by credentials that speak directly to the training and experience related to the job title itself.[2] A corporation simply does not hire those talented in communication skills if it thinks the jobs call for preparation in business administration, engineering, computer science, and accounting. At this stage, the ability to communicate is either taken for granted or is regarded as only one of a number of personal qualities and skills being sought. It is only after the

---

[2] Corporations, it needs to be said, are always interested in how well applicants "project" themselves, a projection that involves in part a capacity to verbalize. But the judgment really rests on a whole spectrum of personality factors—appearance, manners, seriousness of purpose, self-control, and so forth.

applicants have been hired and have gone to work that their ability to communicate well becomes a factor in their success, in what is called their upward mobility in the corporation. For aspiring corporate types, the moment of truth usually comes not at the beginning but a bit later, when the corporation takes a special interest in the performance of potential future managers.

The corporation takes such an interest because it knows that no matter what their special responsibility, managers will spend a great deal of time communicating. Even though their ability to do so with precision and speed will not determine their success, it will certainly play a part. Corporations are not run by simple yes-and-no verbal decisions, any more than are academic or governmental groups. Corporate decisions are reached by procedures of documentation and consultation, by prepared statements and oral presentations. Though politics and personal wishes may be involved, these are usually worked into the documentations and presentations clearly enough to be visible, where they can be accounted for. Managers who are not accustomed to careful communication will feel insecure with their more literate peers, and though they may not fall off the corporate ladder, they will find its rungs a bit shaky.

So it appears that justice finally finds its way to English teachers. But the justice is more poetic than real. A few managers who communicate well may give credit to their early teachers. But they are exceptions, very modest liberal-arts types, with long and amiable memories. The others tend to credit their training in applied sciences ("it taught me how to think"), or their natural genius, or self-study and discipline. Several of my corporate colleagues say they wish they had taken "more English and speech" in college or had applied themselves more in high school, but I regard the comment mostly as an attempt on their part to say something they think I want to hear. Managers who communicate well have educational backgrounds that vary considerably. If they have anything in common besides their experience in the corporation and being bright types generally, it is the practice of reading a good deal, with a critical eye. But this is a personal, temperamental characteristic, neither encouraged nor discouraged by the corporation.

For the truth is that, until very recently, the corporation has done very little, formally, beyond recognizing the importance of communicating well to its operating efficiency. I mean "formally" in the sense of structurally—organizing itself so as to be more certain than it is of selecting employees who can read and write and speak well, or establishing programs to train them to do it. The corporation frequently hires consultants in writing and speaking to help their managers. But the concern is short-winded, the interest easily distracted. To help with specific programs— speeches, presentations, panels—there is almost always the corporation speech writer or coach (who is usually someone in public or press relations). Though a corporate manager may say he wants only ideas or "rough drafts" from speech writers (and though he may be quite able to draft his own presentations), he really expects the corporation speech writers to give him a finished product. He would like to write the speech, but he "hasn't time," he will say. What he means is that he can't or won't shut off the phone or delay his appointment schedule while he takes the time necessary for a long piece of writing. An unfriendly critic would say that he lacks the essential self-discipline; a friendly one would say that he manages his priorities in a different way from writers. Whichever, given the demands, real or imagined, on his time, he finds it less frustrating to order the writing done and then hope the speech coaches will make it sound like himself.

The professional corporate communicators, who know the inherent relationship between substance and style, between personality and expression, get anxious about the propriety of such arrangements. They are aware that academic English teachers flunk those students who put forth another's writing as their own; and they suspect that it is this difference that helps make adversaries of the teaching and corporate worlds. But if they do suspect it, they overstate the importance. In the day-in day-out operation of the corporation, the corporate speech writer/coach is not pervasively important. This person's task is for special occasions. The operating letters, reports, and other directives are actually composed by managers, from first-level supervisors to senior officers. These compositions, which may be given orally, are summaries or reviews of actions, recommendations for new ways-of-going, responses to proposals, and policy statements themselves. Though they may be edited (diplomatically) by an administrative secretary or assistant or subordinate, they are mostly written by the persons who sign them. By and large, only these persons have the understanding and knowledge of the specific circumstances at hand to do the writing. Only they can assemble the facts so as to order up properly the sentences that make up the letter or the report or the speech.

It is at this point that communications teachers will recognize the real-life example of what they have been saying over and over again in the classroom, where they and the corporate communicators at last stand on common ground: what makes the world move really *is* reading and writing and speaking.

The recognition by both corporations and teachers of such a common ground is not in itself new. It is rather the recent emphasis given to this recognition, first by corporations seeking a more structured way to teach, or reteach, communication skills; and second by communications teachers facing the curricular demands of the career education movement. The chief problem for corporations is to develop a program that will be quickly effective with busy employees. The chief problem for teachers is, as always, student motivation: how to make students see that skill in communication will increase their chances for success, not simply in school or college, but in work-a-day life. What teachers have on their side are the training and resources to do the job well. What corporations have, on the other hand, is the essential requirement of doing the job successfully—that is, highly motivated students. How to get the training and the resources together with the motivation will help determine both the definition and the success of career education in English.

On Keeping One's Options Open

Edmund J. Farrell
University of Texas at Austin

In a highly personal and flavorful style, the author stresses the necessity and desirability of adaptability as a goal for career education. Career education is implicitly defined as a lifelong process, not as a one-shot preparatory program. Many suggestions are offered for language arts experiences that could help students learn to anticipate and deal with change.

Persons born into the twentieth century need neither a Bob Dylan to tell them that "the times they are a-changing" nor an Alvin Toffler to inform them that the present does not hold. Relentlessly swept into futures not of their making at speeds that leave them intellectually benumbed and emotionally exhausted, they are double kin to Lady Macbeth, feeling with her the future in the instant and, like that unfortunate aspiring spouse, discovering only too late that their "best-laid schemes . . . gang aft a-gley."

Consider: an adult in 1900 was dependent primarily on horse and buggy for local transportation; had never heard a radio or viewed television; had never flown in an airplane or seen a computer; had never worn synthetic materials or been vaccinated against polio or measles; had not heard of quantum theory, theories of relatively, or atomic and hydrogen bombs; was unfamiliar with Sigmund Freud and psychoanalysis; had never been subjected to a standardized IQ test; had not attended a sound motion picture or peered through an electron microscope; had never been treated with penicillin or Aureomycin; had not seen a vacuum tube or a transistor; had not fought in or borne witness to two world wars and numerous not so minor ones; was unfamiliar with Intelsat, Comsat, and the United Nations; had never read the Brown Decision or heard of Martin Luther King; could not have defined OPEC or intelligently argued for or against nuclear

122

energy; had never held an automatic rifle, been caught speeding in a radar trap, or aimed a laser beam at anyone for any reason.

In 1900 the average citizen aged twenty-one had approximately eight years of education. During those eight years, no class time had been given to discussions of the civil rights movement, the women's liberation movement, the American Indian movement, *la raza*, or black nationalism. Not yet matters of educational import were such phenomena as agribusiness, DNA and RNA, walks on the moon, transmitted pictures of far distant planets, divorce rates, single-parent households, legalized abortion, artificial insemination, *in vitro* fertilization, international tourism, birth-control pills, intrauterine devices, vasectomies, brain implants, transplanted kidneys or hearts, socialized medicine, legalized pornography, double-digit inflation, mind-altering drugs, electronic surveillance of citizens, neutron bombs, military-industrial complexes, multinational business conglomerates, hand calculators, credit-card industries, ecumenical movements, diplomatic recognition of China, or SALT agreements.

As one born into times somewhat quieter than the present, I was privileged as a youth to find no shortage of work or of jobs. My brother, my sister, and I were responsible for a cluster of chores, some required of each of us daily ("Pick up your room and make your bed"), some assigned on a rotating basis ("Clear the table and do the dishes," "Scrub the kitchen floor," "Dust the front room"), some determined by greater strength or at least lesser susceptibility to hay fever ("Cut the lawn"). The work I did around the house was work for which I was not paid, at least not directly. It was the contribution each of us children made to the maintenance of our household and family.

The jobs I held outside our home were numerous, and the income they provided went to buying my clothes, supporting the household budget, and furnishing me a modest allowance. By the time I was twenty-three, I had had experience as a prune picker, pin setter, bellhop, stock boy, warehouseman, clothes seller, brewery worker, disbursing storekeeper in the U.S. Navy, and census taker. I have muscle memory of kneeling on clods under a burning sun and picking prunes until I was too weary by nightfall to lift my fork for dinner. I know what it is to unload boxcars and shift freight by hand truck, and to jump in and out of the dusty pits of bowling alleys and hand-set pins with indigent winos on both sides of me. I have had beer bottles explode in my hand after they had been weakened by the heat of the pasteurizer, and as a census taker I was both sexually propositioned and threatened with my life.

The work I have done, the jobs I have held, have enriched my days and, I would like to believe, my teaching. But always as a youth I knew that the work would come to an end in time, that the jobs were responsibilities of the moment, means to some further educational end, not lifetime commitments.

On the whole, my short-term view has served me well Orchards in which I once picked prunes have long since been leveled for housing tracts; bowling alleys and brewery rooms are now automated; hydraulic equipment and crated goods have displaced thousands of warehouse workers; and census taking is at best an infrequent occupation.

Through no fault of their own, my nine and eleven-year-old sons are deprived, for they have the possessions of affluence without the sense of satisfaction that comes from making significant contributions to the running of a household and from earning money regularly from jobs held outside the home. Though my wife and I have assigned them chores, electricity and gasoline make mockery of much of their labor: like most of mid-class America, we have dishwasher and dryer, vacuum cleaner in place of carpet sweeper, gasoline-powered lawn mower, and electrically charged Weed Eater. Both unions and age deny my children the kinds of employment once available to me. Unfortunately, one learns little about the dignity of work and the pride that accompanies a job well done by being told to stack plates in the dishwasher and carry out the garbage daily.

I endorse any movement that inculcates in young people appreciation for the work carried on by others and esteem for the work they themselves undertake. If the movement can arrange for them part-time jobs for pay, so much the better. In fact, if I had my way, every student—male or female—would learn the skills necessary for running a household as well as those necessary for becoming initially employable. In recent years, I have concluded, perhaps simplistically, that the war between the sexes is one precipitated largely by fear: because they have never learned to cook, run washing machines, buy groceries, and get kids off to school, most husbands grow unhealthily dependent upon their wives and harbor unexpressed fears of desertion through death or divorce; because they have not been on the labor market for years and regard themselves as unemployable, many wives come to view their husbands as "sole breadwinner" and share similar fears of being left alone to cope. Any human relationship in which individuals do not feel adequately self-sufficient to survive its termination with grace is a relationship in trouble, one in which anger—not always suppressed—can be found at the core. As therapists attest, two strong *I*'s make a strong *we*.

While I favor students' having both book and hands-on knowledge about the world of work, while I want young people to master the social and academic skills necessary for their becoming employable, while I want members of both sexes to feel competent to take charge of their own lives, I do not want schools to foster the notion that the individual, the society, or the world has been, is, or ever will be in stasis.

The first job held is rarely the last held. Jobs come and go, according to the vagaries of the marketplace and advances in technology. Fifteen years ago, Grant Venn reported that automatic elevators displaced 40,000 elevator operators in New York City alone, that new equipment in the Census Bureau enabled 50 statisticians to do the work in 1960 that required 4,000 in 1950, that the check-writing staff in the Treasury Department had been reduced from 400 people to 4.[1] Thirteen years ago Arnold Barach pointed out that in less than fifteen years, 3,000,000 workers had been replaced by machines in coal mines, over 130,000 had been made surplus in steel mills, and that 10 men, using automated equipment, were able to do the work of a previous 400 in producing auto motor blocks.[2]

Students need to learn to anticipate changes, in both themselves and the nature of work, which may occur over the span of their lives; further, they need to learn what resources are available should they desire to alter the pattern of either their employment or their leisure-time activities. In English classes, students might read and discuss traditional and contemporary selections, fictive and nonfictive, in which work and its effects on characters' lives are prominent concerns. (Dickens, Lawrence, Orwell, Hardy, Flaubert, Blazac, Cather, Tolstoy, Twain, Howells, Melville, Norris, as well as Studs Terkel, Jules Lester, Tillie Olsen, Ernest Gaines, Sloan Wilson, Harriet Arnow, Oscar Lewis, Maya Angelou, John McPhee, Eve Curie, Roger Angell, Harvey Swados, and Agnes De Mille faintly suggest how widely one could range.) Students might also read and discuss speculative fiction—dystopian and utopian literature, since fiction and science fantasy—for the imaginative insights into possible futures of the society such literature offers. To encourage them to create worthy goals for potential societal futures, students might be divided into groups, each of which is responsible for planning its own American utopia.

To help them perceive themselves and the society as being in continuous process, students might be asked to describe in detail what they anticipate to be a typical day in their lives at ages thirty, fifty, and seventy-five. Similarly, they might be asked to assume that, at age seventy-five, they are to respond to a grandchild's request to describe the most important events in their lives. To help them appreciate some of the responsibilities borne by persons in different walks of life, they might be invited to role play via the following kinds of assignments.

a. Assume that you have decided to campaign for local mayor. Write a statement describing what you intend to do to improve your city.

b. Assume that you are a medical doctor and that three of your patients have a terminal kidney disease. You have a machine available for the dialysis of only one person. Discuss the criteria by which you decide which patient shall live.

c. Assume that you are a teacher and that you discover that one of your favorite students has been cheating regularly on tests. Outline the procedures you would take to alter the student's behavior.

d. Assume that you are an electrician and that you have been told to install in new homes wiring you believe to be defective. If you challenge your employer, chances are that you will be fired. If you install the wiring, chances are that eventually a home will burn. You are not sure you can get another job, and you need money. Describe what you would do and why you would do it.

But enough. Within an English class, opportunities appear limitless for increasing students' knowledge about the world of work, for expanding their imaginations by engaging them creatively in their own possible futures, and for having them empathetically endure the responsibility of making the kinds of work-a-day decisions that confront individuals in various occupations.

What students should receive from counselors and other teachers is information about the opportunities available to continue to grow intellectually and emotionally regardless of their initial occupations. Self-determined programs of home reading; extension courses; universities without walls; nonresidential colleges; diverse late afternoon and evening programs, both academic and cultural, on local campuses; videotape and sound cassettes for home viewing and listening; programs on computer; courses sponsored by businesses and industries—myriad are the ways one can continue to learn.

Because I sputtered my way into English teaching after a number of false starts, I balk at encouraging any young person to make a premature closure on a career, particularly since every vocation, including that of English teaching, undergoes constant if not dramatic change. Now post-fifty, I feel that I am still learning, still becoming, still desirous of keeping my options open, still unsure of what I may be tomorrow, next week, next year. May it always be thus—for me, for you, and for those we teach.

Notes

1. Grant Venn, *Man, Education, and Work* (Washington: American Council on Education).

2. Arnold Barach, "Changing Technology and Changing Culture," in *Automation, Education, and Human Values*, ed. William Brickman and Stanley Lehrer (New York: School and Society Books, 1966).

Contributors

Reta F. Broadway is Field Representative for the Newspaper in Education Program at *The Courier-Journal* and *The Louisville Times*. In this position, she serves as a consultant to teachers who use the newspaper in their classrooms. She has taught social studies, reading, and English in both middle school and high school. She has developed curriculum materials for teachers who wish to use the newspaper to help integrate career education concepts into the teaching of their subject.

Dorothy C. Davidson is Associate Commissioner for General Education in the Texas Education Agency where she has been employed in various positions since 1954. Davidson represented NCTE at two national conferences on career education in 1974 and 1977 and chaired a preconvention study group, "English Language Arts and Career Education," at the annual NCTE convention in 1977. She is a co-author of the essay, "Career Education in the English Classroom" in the book *Career Education in the Academic Classroom*. She is an active member of IRA, NCTE, ASSEARS, and ASCD.

James S. Davis is a Specialist Consultant in Secondary Language Arts and Reading at the Grant Wood Area Education Agency in Cedar Rapids, Iowa. A former high school and college teacher of English and an English educator, Davis has been active in both the Missouri and Iowa affiliates of NCTE. He is currently the president of the Iowa Council of Teachers of English and is active in national level activities of CEE, CSSEDC, and ALAN.

Mildred A. Dougherty, a former secondary and college teacher of English, has been an English and reading supervisor and curriculum consultant for the Jefferson County, Kentucky, Public Schools since 1966. The Greater Kentucky Council of Teachers of English recently honored her for her service with the establishment of the Mildred A. Dougherty Award for the Outstanding Communicator in Kentucky. In recent years, Dougherty has been involved in curriculum consulting and textbook writing and editing and has been active in KCTE, GLCTE, NCTE, and IRA. Her involvement in career education began when she was one of five persons to represent NCTE at the conference, Career Education for the Academic Classroom, held at the University of Maryland in December 1974. She co-authored "Career Education in the English Classroom," which became an essay in the book produced as a result of the conference, *Career Education in the Academic Classroom*.

Marjorie N. Farmer, a member of the NCTE Task Force on Career Education, is a former middle school, high school, and college teacher of English and an English educator. Past president of NCTE (1978-1979), she has been active in NCTE as well as IRA, ALA, ASCD, and SCA. She has served many educational associations, agencies, and projects as a consultant on reading, composition, and literature. Farmer was one of several persons to represent NCTE at national conferences on career education in 1974 and 1977, and she is co-author of the essay, "Career Education in the English Classroom," in the book *Career Education in the Academic Classroom.*

Edmund J. Farrell, a former secondary and college teacher of English and an English educator, is currently Professor of English Education at the University of Texas at Austin. A member of the NCTE Task Force on Career Education, Farrell is also a past president of the California Association of Teachers of English and a former Associate Executive Director of NCTE (1970-1978). He has served on numerous NCTE committees and commissions, including the Commission on Literature and the Executive Committee of CEE. He has written and edited numerous English textbooks, including his latest works, *Purpose in Literature* and *Arrangement in Literature.* He has published over 33 articles in national magazines and journals, and is the author of *Deciding the Future: A Forecast of Responsibilities of Secondary Teachers of English, 1970-2000 A.D.*

Marjorie M. Kaiser, the editor of this book, is currently Assistant Professor of Education at the University of Louisville and a member of the NCTE Task Force on Career Education. A former middle school and high school teacher and supervisor of English teachers, Kaiser is active in KCTE, GLCTE, and NCTE. She is currently a member of the NCTE Committee to Revise *Books For You: A Booklist for Senior High Students.* Kaiser's research and publications have focused on the subjects of adolescent literature and career education. In May of 1977, she was recognized for commendable research in education by the Virginia Educational Research Association. Her interest in English and career education has been most evident in her work as a curriculum consultant and presenter of papers at local, state, and national conferences, and in her publications in *Language Arts, The Virginia English Bulletin,* and *The Journal of Career Education.* In addition, she has written a doctoral dissertation on the subject of English and career education.

Jan E. Kilby, Director of the NCTE Project on Career Education at the National Council of Teachers of English, is a former high school and college teacher of English and an English educator. Kilby completed her doctoral dissertation on the subject of English and career education. Her professional activities and publications reflect her interest in the college teaching of English, career education, and counseling and guidance. She is currently serving as a member of the Advisory Board of the Career Education Project of the American Personnel and Guidance Association, for whom she is completing an issue paper entitled *School Counselor Collaboration with Teachers and Other Education Personnel in the Delivery of Career Education.* She is the editor of the book *Career Education and English, K-12: Ideas for the Classroom,* the companion to this volume.

Glenn Leggett, a member of the NCTE Task Force on Career Education, is recently retired from his position as Vice President for Corporate Communications at Deere and Company. His professional experiences include positions as professor of English and university provost and president. Leggett is the recipient of numerous honorary doctoral degrees and has been professionally active in MLA, NCTE, and CEEB. He has published numerous articles, reviews, and books on the topics of higher education and English, and was just recently the recipient of the Edward S. Noyes Award for distinguished service to education and the College Board, given by the College Entrance Examination Board.

Alan Lemke, Assistant Professor of English and Education at the University of Nebraska at Lincoln, is a former secondary and college teacher and supervisor of English teachers, an English educator, and a curriculum consultant in English in a state education agency. He has several publications on the topics of language and composition and recently assisted in editing a special series of monographs on the language arts for the Illinois Office of Education.

Beatrice J. Levin is Assistant Director for Reading and English for the School District of Philadelphia. Active in NCTE, APA, and IRA, Levin has been a high school teacher and supervisor of English and reading and is a certified speech therapist and school psychologist. She is the author of *Real Life Reading Skills: A Scholastic Program in Functional Literacy* and numerous other articles and books.

Alan McLeod, editor of the *Virginia English Bulletin*, is an Associate Professor of Education at Virginia Commonwealth University where he has taught for ten years. McLeod has been extremely active in a variety of roles in NCTE, CEE, and VATE during these years. Since 1975, he has been involved in career education efforts in Virginia, both statewide and within his university.

Roger Nall is a career education consultant at the Grand Wood Area Education Agency in Cedar Rapids, Iowa. He has had extensive experience working with teachers of all subject areas in integrating career education into the K-12 curriculum.

Jesse Perry, a member of the NCTE Task Force on Career Education, is Language Arts Specialist for the San Diego City Schools. Perry has been an active member of NCTE, serving as a member of the Commission on Literature, the committee that produced *Books for You: A Booklist for Senior High Students* in 1976, and the SLATE Steering Committee. He is a former teacher and supervisor of English teachers at the secondary and college levels and an English educator, as well as an administrator and consultant on many educational projects. Perry was one of five persons to represent NCTE at a national conference on career education in December 1974 and he is a co-author of "Career Education in the English Classroom," an essay in *Career Education in the Academic Classroom* produced as a result of the conference. Perry is currently a very active member of numerous state and national organizations for supervisors, teachers, and administrators.

Richard E. Roberts is a teacher of English at Arlington Senior High School in Poughkeepsie, New York. He has taught middle school and high school English, as well as English as a second language. Roberts was responsible for developing the senior English elective, Career English, which has been taught in his school since the fall of 1973 and which was the subject of his article, "Career Investigation and Planning in the High School English Curriculum" in the November 1978 issue of *English Journal*. He is currently preparing a secondary English textbook entitled *Putting English to Work for Work*.

Patricia Read Russell is an Associate Professor of English at Stephen F. Austin State University in Nacogdoches, Texas. She has had professional experience in higher education as a teacher of English and administrative intern and has taught numerous English courses, including literature for children. She is active in NCTE, CEA, SCMLA, and AAUW and has recently been involved in on-campus activities relating to the career education of women students and the preprofessional preparation of students in several disciplines.

Robert Shenk is currently a member of the Department of English at the United States Air Force Academy. A former communications officer for the U.S. Navy and a college teacher of English, Shenk has for the past few years devoted his research and several conference presentations and articles to the theme of vocation in literature and has taught composition courses integrating images of vocation in literature. He is in the process of developing a high school literature anthology focusing on themes of vocation in literature and has presented a paper on "Richard McKenna's *Sand Pebbles* and the Poetry of Machinery" at *Interface* '79, the third annual Humanities and Technology Conference sponsored by the Southern Technical Institute, October 1979. Shenk was a consultant/speaker at the 1979 NCTE preconvention workshop, "Career Education in the English Program K-12," where he shared his innovative approach of examining career education concepts in literature.

Robert C. Small, Jr., is Associate Dean of Graduate Studies and Research, Virginia Polytechnic Institute and State University. He is co-editor of *Literature for Adolescents* and author of *The New Fiction* and *View Point and Point of View*, as well as the author of articles in *Language Arts, English Journal, English Education*, and other journals. His article "Censorship and English" recently appeared in *Dealing with Censorship*, published by NCTE. He is a director of the NCTE Assembly on Literature for Adolescents (1977–present) and an active participant in VATE, CEE, and NCTE. He is also a department editor for the *Virginia English Bulletin* and chair of the NCTE Committee to Revise *Books for You*. In addition, Small has presented several papers and conducted workshops on the topic of career education.

Charles Suhor, Deputy Executive Director for Professional Programs at NCTE, is a former English teacher and supervisor for the New Orleans Public Schools, where he worked on several career education projects. In the past he has served in numerous NCTE groups and the New Orleans and Louisiana affiliates of NCTE. A prolific writer, editor, and poet, Suhor's writings have appeared in *English Journal, Media and Methods, Learning, College Composition and Communication, English Education,* and the *Journal of Career Education.* He edits the "NCTE to You" portions of the three NCTE section journals and has written high school textbooks on composition and literature. Suhor represented NCTE at a 1977 U.S. Office of Education conference on career education and has written articles on English and career education.

Seymour Yesner, now Director of English Language Arts for the Brookline, Massachusetts, Public Schools, was Consultant in English and Humanities, K-12, for the Minneapolis Public Schools from 1971-1979. Prior to this position, he was a secondary and college teacher of English, both in the United States and in Thailand, where he was a Fulbright lecturer. Active in NCTE, CEE, and many other educational associations, Yesner has had a distinguished career as an expert in English and the humanities, serving as a consultant, speaker, and evaluator of the programs and publications of various agencies, school districts, and associations. He has been especially active with the National Endowment for the Humanities. He also serves as a reader for several major publishers of English language arts textbooks.